Journey to Freedom

A STUDY ON THE LIFE OF MOSES

KYRA DANIELS

Study Suggestions

We believe that the Bible is true, trustworthy, and timeless and that it is vitally important for all believers. These study suggestions are intended to help you more effectively study Scripture as you seek to know and love God through His Word.

SUGGESTED STUDY TOOLS

- ○ A Bible

- ○ A double-spaced, printed copy of the Scripture passages that this study covers. You can use a website like *www.biblegateway.com* to copy the text of a passage and print out a double-spaced copy to be able to mark on easily.

- ○ A journal to write notes or prayers

- ○ Pens, colored pencils, and highlighters

- ○ A dictionary to look up unfamiliar words

HOW TO USE THIS STUDY

Begin your study time in prayer. Ask God to reveal Himself to you, to help you understand what you are reading, and to transform you with His Word (Psalm 119:18).

Before you read what is written in each day of the study itself, read the assigned passages of Scripture for that day. Use your double-spaced copy to circle, underline, highlight, draw arrows, and mark in any way you would like to help you dig deeper as you work through a passage.

Read the daily written content provided for the current study day.

Answer the questions that appear at the end of each study day.

HOW TO STUDY THE BIBLE

The inductive method provides tools for deeper and more intentional Bible study. To study a book of the Bible inductively, work through the steps below after reading background information on the book.

1 OBSERVATION & COMPREHENSION
Key question: What does the text say?

After reading the book of the Bible in its entirety at least once, begin working with smaller portions of the book. Read a passage of Scripture repetitively, and then mark the following items in the text:

- Key or repeated words and ideas
- Key themes
- Transition words (*Ex: therefore, but, because, if/then, likewise, etc.*)
- Lists
- Comparisons & Contrasts
- Commands
- Unfamiliar words (look these up in a dictionary)
- Questions you have about the text

2 INTERPRETATION
Key question: What does the text mean?

Once you have annotated the text, work through the following steps to help you interpret its meaning:

- Read the passage in other versions for a better understanding of the text.
- Read cross-references to help interpret Scripture with Scripture.
- Paraphrase or summarize the passage to check for understanding.
- Identify how the text reflects the metanarrative of Scripture, which is the story of creation, fall, redemption, and restoration.
- Read trustworthy commentaries if you need further insight into the meaning of the passage.

3 APPLICATION
Key Question: How should the truth of this passage change me?

Bible study is not merely an intellectual pursuit. The truths about God, ourselves, and the gospel that we discover in Scripture should produce transformation in our hearts and lives. Answer the following questions as you consider what you have learned in your study:

- What attributes of God's character are revealed in the passage?

  Consider places where the text directly states the character of God, as well as how His character is revealed through His words and actions.

- What do I learn about myself in light of who God is?

  Consider how you fall short of God's character, how the text reveals your sin nature, and what it says about your new identity in Christ.

- How should this truth change me?

  A passage of Scripture may contain direct commands telling us what to do or warnings about sins to avoid in order to help us grow in holiness. Other times our application flows out of seeing ourselves in light of God's character. As we pray and reflect on how God is calling us to change in light of His Word, we should be asking questions like, "How should I pray for God to change my heart?" and "What practical steps can I take toward cultivating habits of holiness?"

ATTRIBUTES OF GOD

ETERNAL

God has no beginning and no end. He always was, always is, and always will be.

HAB. 1:12 / REV. 1:8 / IS. 41:4

FAITHFUL

God is incapable of anything but fidelity. He is loyally devoted to His plan and purpose.

2 TIM. 2:13 / DEUT. 7:9
HEB. 10:23

GLORIOUS

God is ultimately beautiful, deserving of all praise and honor.

REV. 19:1 / PS. 104:1
EX. 40:34-35

GOOD

God is pure; there is no defilement in Him. He is unable to sin, and all He does is good.

GEN. 1:31 / PS. 34:8 / PS. 107:1

GRACIOUS

God is kind, giving to us gifts and benefits which we do not deserve.

2 KINGS 13:23 / PS. 145:8
IS. 30:18

HOLY

God is undefiled and unable to be in the presence of defilement. He is sacred and set-apart.

REV. 4:8 / LEV. 19:2 / HAB. 1:13

IMMUTABLE

God does not change. He is the same yesterday, today, and tomorrow.

1 SAM. 15:29 / ROM. 11:29
JAMES 1:17

JEALOUS

God is desirous of receiving the praise and affection He rightly deserves.

EX. 20:5 / DEUT. 4:23-24
JOSH. 24:19

JUST

God governs in perfect justice. He acts in accordance with justice. In Him there is no wrongdoing or dishonesty.

IS. 61:8 / DEUT. 32:4 / PS. 146:7-9

LOVE

God is eternally, enduringly, steadfastly loving and affectionate. He does not forsake or betray His covenant love.

JN. 3:16 / EPH. 2:4-5 / 1 JN. 4:16

MERCIFUL

God is compassionate, withholding us from the wrath that we deserve.

TITUS 3:5 / PS. 25:10
LAM. 3:22-23

OMNIPOTENT

God is all-powerful; His strength is unlimited.

MAT. 19:26 / JOB 42:1-2
JER. 32:27

OMNIPRESENT

God is everywhere; His presence is near and permeating.

PROV. 15:3 / PS. 139:7-10
JER. 23:23-24

OMNISCIENT

God is all-knowing; there is nothing unknown to Him.

PS. 147:4 / I JN. 3:20
HEB. 4:13

PATIENT

God is long-suffering and enduring. He gives ample opportunity for people to turn toward Him.

ROM. 2:4 / 2 PET. 3:9 / PS. 86:15

RIGHTEOUS

God is blameless and upright. There is no wrong found in Him.

PS. 119:137 / JER. 12:1
REV. 15:3

SOVEREIGN

God governs over all things; He is in complete control.

COL. 1:17 / PS. 24:1-2
1 CHRON. 29:11-12

TRUE

God is our measurement of what is fact. By Him are we able to discern true and false.

JN. 3:33 / ROM. 1:25 / JN. 14:6

WISE

God is infinitely knowledgeable and is judicious with His knowledge.

IS. 46:9-10 / IS. 55:9 / PROV. 3:19

Creation

In the beginning, God created the universe. He made the world and everything in it. He created humans in His own image to be His representatives on the earth.

Fall

The first humans, Adam and Eve, disobeyed God by eating from the fruit of the Tree of Knowledge of Good and Evil. Because of sin, the world was cursed. The punishment for sin is death, and because of Adam's original sin, all humans are sinful and condemned to death.

Redemption

God sent his Son to become a human and redeem His people. Jesus Christ lived a sinless life but died on the cross to pay the penalty for sin. He resurrected from the dead and ascended into heaven. All who put their faith in Jesus are saved from death and freely receive the gift of eternal life.

Restoration

One day, Jesus Christ will return again and restore all that sin destroyed. He will usher in a new heaven and new earth where all who trust in Him will live eternally with glorified bodies in the presence of God.

TIMELINE OF SCRIPTURE

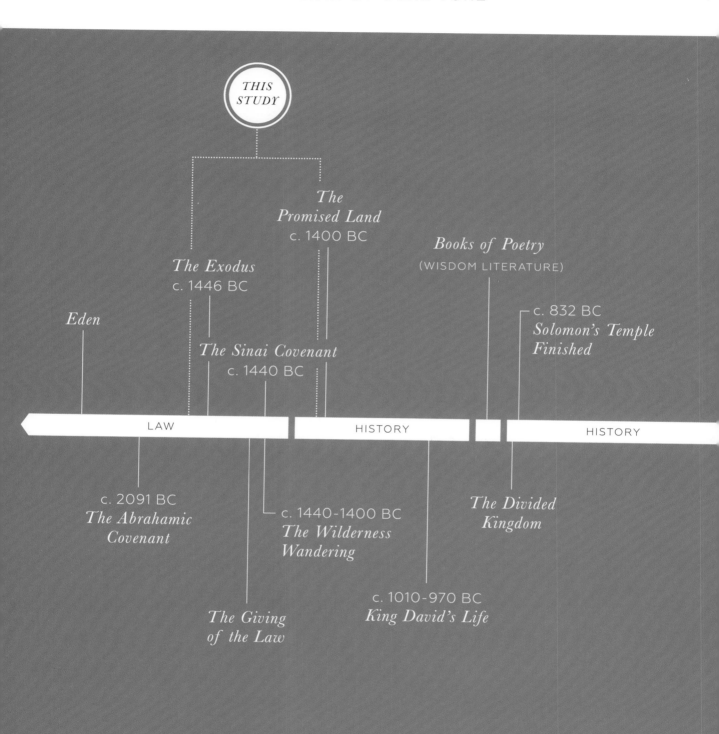

THIS STUDY

Eden

The Exodus
c. 1446 BC

The Sinai Covenant
c. 1440 BC

The Promised Land
c. 1400 BC

Books of Poetry
(WISDOM LITERATURE)

c. 832 BC
Solomon's Temple Finished

LAW

HISTORY

HISTORY

c. 2091 BC
The Abrahamic Covenant

c. 1440-1400 BC
The Wilderness Wandering

The Giving of the Law

c. 1010-970 BC
King David's Life

The Divided Kingdom

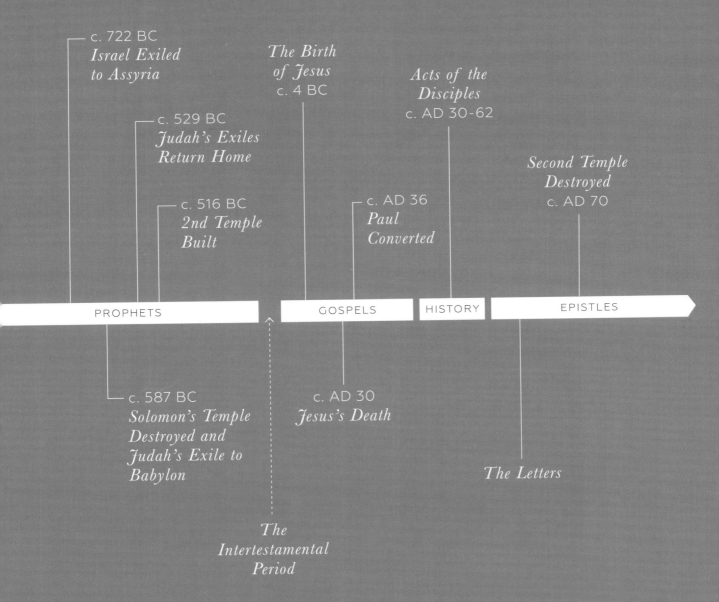

c. 722 BC
*Israel Exiled
to Assyria*

c. 529 BC
*Judah's Exiles
Return Home*

c. 516 BC
*2nd Temple
Built*

*The Birth
of Jesus*
c. 4 BC

*Acts of the
Disciples*
c. AD 30-62

*Second Temple
Destroyed*
c. AD 70

c. AD 36
*Paul
Converted*

PROPHETS   **GOSPELS**   **HISTORY**   **EPISTLES**

c. 587 BC
*Solomon's Temple
Destroyed and
Judah's Exile to
Babylon*

c. AD 30
Jesus's Death

The Letters

*The
Intertestamental
Period*

contents

WEEK FOUR

WEEK FIVE

WEEK SIX

WEEK SEVEN

JOURNEY TO FREEDOM

Adopted Yet Out of Place

WEEK ONE

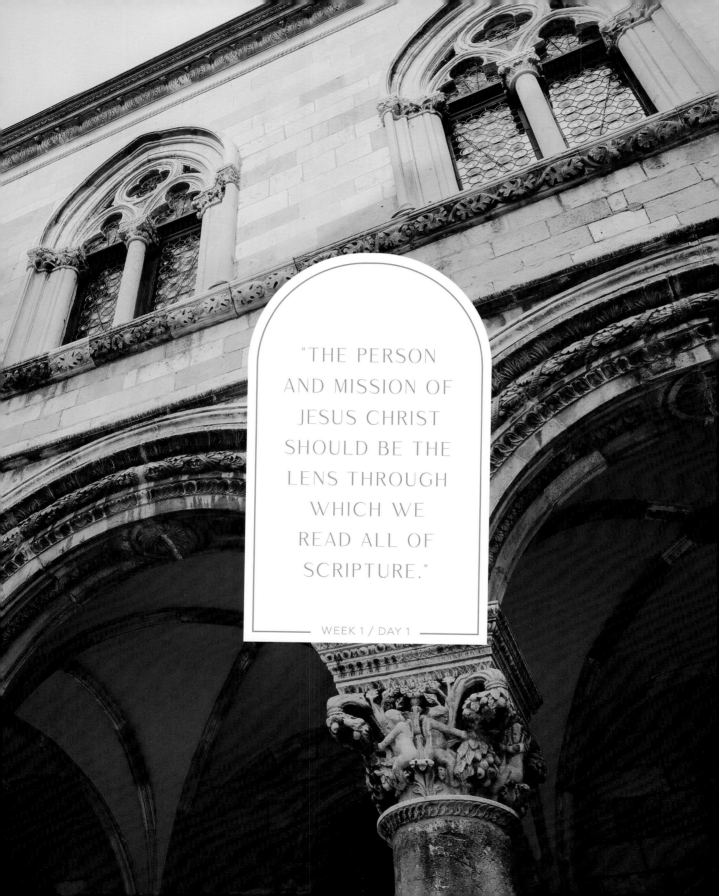

"THE PERSON
AND MISSION OF
JESUS CHRIST
SHOULD BE THE
LENS THROUGH
WHICH WE
READ ALL OF
SCRIPTURE."

WEEK 1 / DAY 1

Introduction to the Life of Moses

From Charlton Heston in *The Ten Commandments* to Disney's *Prince of Egypt*, the life of Moses has been depicted throughout the decades. People are intrigued by this man's incredible story, which involves genocide, slavery, refugees, and war. Through the hardships, God is evident in Moses's life as Moses works in the Lord's plan to bring redemption. But, each stage of his journey leaves us longing for a redeemer to resolve sin and accomplish God's plan completely. Moses is a picture of the promises fulfilled in Jesus Christ, and this study will explore the relationship between the two. We will take an in-depth look at typology, a concept that identifies people, events, and symbols in the Old Testament as representations of divine truth realized in Christ. The people, roles, sacrifices, and festivals of ancient Israel were how the gospel of Jesus was present in hidden form (Colossians 2:17). Typology also highlights the limitations of these symbols and exposes biblical character flaws to show our need for Jesus. Through biblical narrative and other storytelling elements, *Journey to Freedom: A Study on the Life of Moses* studies Moses's birth, mission, service, and death as circumstances that point to the coming of Jesus Christ and the bold revelation of the gospel in its full glory.

Each week, you will read through passages from Exodus to Deuteronomy. Moses is the author of these Old Testament books, so these passages are not only God's word to the Israelites but also autobiographical as Moses records his own life. The disciples' accounts of Jesus in Matthew and John will connect to these sections later in the week. As you are reading the selected passages, note differences and similarities between Moses and Jesus, pay attention to ways you see the need for a deliverer through Moses's life, and observe how Jesus offers this complete deliverance.

Hebrews 3:1-6 presents a framework to approach this typology study. The biblical author calls believers to view Jesus as supreme. The person and mission of Jesus Christ should be the lens through which we read all of Scripture. Hebrews declares Him as our High Priest. Jesus is the mediator between us and God the Father. By His death and resurrection, the eternal Son of God has paid the debt of our rebellion, freed us from slavery to sin, and bestowed on us His righteousness. He has restored our relationship with God because He alone was perfectly faithful and obedient to the Lord's will. The passage continues to juxtapose Jesus and Moses. As a preview of the coming Jesus, Moses acted as mediator and proto-priest for the ancient Israelites. He delivered them from slavery in Egypt and led them into the presence of God on Mount Sinai. He gave them the law of God so that they would be a set apart community and able to worship in the Promised Land. By God's grace, Moses was faithful to the Lord. But Moses was still imperfect, disobedient, and weak at times, and this would be the reason that the life of Moses points to a better One — One who would fulfill these roles perfectly and without sin.

Jesus has received honor and glory greater than Moses. Jesus reigns as Prophet, Priest, and King. The biblical author uses images of a builder and a house to describe how Jesus surpasses Moses. The church is a community of believers, often referred to as one body (1 Corinthians 12:12) or one temple structure (Ephesians 2:19-22). As God the Son, existing in a coeternal union with God the Father and God the Holy Spirit, Jesus is the one who creates and builds it all. Through His saving work, He has gathered His people and built them up as one entity. Individual believers are united under Christ as our head and stand on Him as our foundation. Though God used Moses to establish His dwelling place and define the church through the law, Moses was not the builder but was himself a part of the house. His efforts were a witness to the builder coming to construct a spiritual temple in the hearts of His people.

Jesus states in John 5:46, "For if you believed Moses, you would believe me, because he wrote about me." As you read about the life of Moses, let yourself be guided by the Holy Spirit, and cling to the promise of Jesus. Since we are members of Jesus's house, let us hope in Christ alone to build us up through His Word. In this study, you will see how Moses was also built up and shaped by the Spirit of Jesus who was always with him. The times of faithfulness and setbacks along Moses's journey will motivate you to persevere in your walk with the Lord and hold firm to Jesus as your true deliverer.

THROUGH THE HARDSHIPS, GOD IS EVIDENT IN MOSES'S LIFE AS MOSES WORKS IN THE LORD'S PLAN TO BRING REDEMPTION.

Write out a prayer, asking God to open your eyes to the truth of who He is and the truth of His Word in this study.

_____

_____

_____

_____

_____

_____

_____

_____

How does the imagery in Hebrews 3:1-6 help you place Jesus and Moses in the proper order?

_____

_____

_____

_____

_____

_____

How do you react to Moses being a fellow member of Jesus's church with you?

_____

_____

_____

_____

_____

_____

_____

"THOUGH OUT OF PLACE IN EGYPT, THE ISRAELITES PROSPER."

WEEK 1 / DAY 2

READ EXODUS 1:1-14

Growth under Oppression and Promise

Gathering all their cattle and possessions, the Israelites, God's chosen people, pack up their lives and leave behind the Promised Land to be outsiders in a foreign territory. Canaan, a land in the ancient Middle East known for its agricultural productivity and bounty, has been overcome by a period of drought and famine. The green and flowering landscape has dried up, wasting away the hope of land for God's beloved. The eleven sons of Jacob lead the small nation of seventy to Egypt. Along the journey, God assures their gray patriarch that He has not forgotten the promise made to his grandfather, Abraham. Jacob remembers the covenant, a binding promise, to which the Lord has committed Himself. According to His earlier word, God will make Abraham's family into a great nation, as numerous as the stars of the sky and sand on the seashore (Genesis 22:17). He will bring them to the land of Canaan, which will be their permanent possession (Genesis 17:8). Others will be blessed through them (Genesis 12:3), and, most importantly, God will be theirs (Genesis 46:4).

Finally, the family of Israel enters the desert land of pyramids, sphinxes, and strange gods. They reunite with the lost son, Joseph, who had been sold into Egyptian slavery by his brothers but through God's protection, was kept and favored by the Egyptian regime. In His foreknowledge, God makes provision for His people through Joseph's position in Pharaoh's court. After Pharaoh's welcome, they feed on Egypt's agricultural reserves and settle in Goshen, an arable area nourished by the Nile River. As time passes, Jacob and Joseph die, but they pass with the hope that God will take the Israelites to the Promised Land again. At the end of Genesis, Joseph tells his family to remember to carry his deceased body on their journey back home.

Though out of place in Egypt, the Israelites prosper. Exodus 1:7 emphasizes their abundance through the repetition of this theme. The text states that "the Israelites were fruitful, increased rapidly, multiplied, and became extremely numerous so that the land was filled with them." God keeps His covenant promise, growing them into a great nation. There is also creation language used with the word "filled." As God commissioned Adam and Eve to fill the earth with image-bearers, the Israelites also engage in this creative mission. Through their presence in Egypt, the Israelites make God's kingdom known.

While the Israelites are flourishing, a new Pharaoh comes to power who does not know about the favored dream interpreter, Joseph, who saved Egypt from famine. In blind leadership, he fails to count the history of the immigrant nation in his empire and looks at them as a burden. From his palace, he sees the strength of the Israelites and becomes concerned that they will overpower the Egyptian regime and escape. Pharaoh is also spiritually blind to God's redemptive work through the Israelites. In his eyes, he creates a wise plan to keep them subdued. As a result, he tries to thwart the divine promises by bringing them under his authoritarian control. Pharaoh institutes slavery upon the Israelites to oppress them and instill fear in their hearts. Pharaoh stands in opposition to God's people and God Himself. Pharaoh is a man in rebellion, becoming an agent of Satan and spiritual evil. But, through His divine foreknowledge, God had seen this slavery coming upon the Israelites when He spoke to Abraham in Genesis 15:13. The four hundred year bondage would play a part in the sovereign will of God, and He would use this dark period to ultimately enact justice on spiritual evil and show His saving faithfulness.

During the strenuous labor, taskmasters watch over the Israelites with whips and sticks in hand, ready to strike at any sign of sloth or dissent. With backs bent, they carry stone and bags of sand. Steeped in mud and clay, the Israelites lay brick upon brick. Through the pain and tears, the Israelites build Pithom and Rameses, great cities for Pharaoh, and the resources of Egypt. The Egyptians make their lives bitter (Exodus 1:14). The people likely become broken down and grieved. Exodus 1:14 continues the style of repetition, but here, the relentless and cruel treatment is emphasized. The whip cracks and blood is shed, but God preserves their numbers and holds their presence in the land. Though the Israelites are under oppression, they are still under the promises of God. God continues the redemptive plan He spoke to Abraham. He will cause them to be a great nation for His kingdom glory.

As we see in today's passage, God continues to grow His people, even in times of suffering and loss. Unfortunate circumstances do not challenge Him. Instead, God uses the wicked plans of men to bring about His good purposes. He sees us through difficulties and always provides the hope and faith we need to persevere in our imperishable relationship with Jesus. In these times, we can trust in Him to grow us and point us to His covenant promises.

THOUGH THE ISRAELITES ARE UNDER OPPRESSION, THEY ARE STILL UNDER THE PROMISES OF GOD.

In this passage, we have seen how God preserved the Israelites through immigration and slavery. What does this reveal about His character?

_____

_____

_____

_____

_____

_____

_____

What does the passage reveal about the reality of spiritual evil that works against the plan of God?

_____

_____

_____

_____

_____

_____

Describe a time when the Lord has grown and strengthened you in times of hardship.

_____

_____

_____

_____

_____

_____

"GOD BRINGS
TO SAFETY THE
BELOVED SON
WHO WILL
DELIVER HIS
PEOPLE."

WEEK 1 / DAY 3

Kept by the Women's Care

Pharaoh peers over his high tower to see a multitude of Israelite slaves. Eyes wide and gripped with anxiety, he worries about a revolt. So, he devises another plan to halt God's covenant promises: death for all of the Israelite boys. Pharaoh attacks the life promised to the people of God. His tactic is sly like the serpent's in the garden of Eden; he tries to subvert from within. He commands the head Hebrew midwives, Shiphrah and Puah, to kill newborn sons. Seeing them as outsiders in his land, Pharaoh uses the term "Hebrew." A name that described their ancestor, Abraham, as he wandered in a foreign land (Genesis 14:13), this term still clings to the Israelite identity as they remain outsiders in Egypt.

Shiphrah and Puah respond with conviction, holding firmly to the fear of the Lord. With hearts set on pleasing God, they defy Pharaoh's edict. They remain loyal to the God of life and promise and do not kill the sons of Israel. Despite his efforts for control, Pharaoh does not have power over God's chosen. In His providence, God softens the women's hearts so they can obey Him for His glory. Likely shocked and frustrated, Pharaoh calls Shiphrah and Puah into his presence. With the Lord on their side, the midwives enter his court and approach the opulent throne of Pharaoh. He questions them about their disobedience. In the face of evil, Shiphrah and Puah mask the truth with a joke, claiming that unlike the Egyptian women, the Hebrew women are in no need of midwifery due to their vigor and strength in labor. Pharaoh is not only beguiled but also ridiculed by two Hebrew women. These women are not coerced by Pharaoh's command and remain faithful to the word of the Lord.

Pharaoh then orders his people to throw every Hebrew boy into the Nile River. The Nile, which was once their source of life in the desert, is now a source of death. Egyptians invade Israelite homes in Goshen and take babies from the care of their mothers. Screaming and weeping fill the land. Satan knows the importance of sons in the nation of Israel and uses Pharaoh's paranoia and pride in an attempt to stop the coming of Israel's Messiah. "Messiah" is a title for the Anointed One who would reign over the nations, establish justice, and destroy sin and evil forever (Genesis 49:10). As that cursed serpent in Eden, Satan is destined to be vanquished by the Messiah, the "seed of the woman" predicted in Genesis 3:15. Fearing the victory of the chosen son, he aims to kill all Hebrew sons through Pharaoh. As the women watch their baby boys sink to the bottom of the river, it seems like Satan's plan has worked. Surely the mothers cry out to God for help. In the silence, all hope seems lost, but God is working to deliver His people through the protection of one son in the tribe of Levi.

God chooses to preserve the son of Jochebed (Exodus 6:20), a Levite woman who has just given birth. He is her innocent, beloved son. When she can no longer hide him, she places him in a basket on the Nile River. Watching the basket travel down the current, perhaps Jochebed hopes her son will float into the hands of an Egyptian woman who will have mercy. The infant boy's older sister, Miriam, follows his path to the bathing area of Pharaoh's daughter. The princess orders her slave to draw the basket from the water. They lift the cover and behold a crying, defenseless child. Immediately, Pharaoh's daughter identifies him as a Hebrew boy, but, unlike her father, she has compassion.

Defying her father's decree, she does not throw him back to the water but brings him to the safety of her arms. Like the midwives, God has softened her heart too, and Pharaoh's authority is mocked again by a woman who cares for the sons of God. Miriam approaches Pharaoh's daughter. Brilliantly, she offers to bring her mother to nurse the boy. Jochebed's relationship with her beloved son is restored, and she raises him during his formative years. After he is weaned, she brings him back to Pharaoh's palace. She knows he will be given opportunities for a better life there. Pharaoh's daughter adopts the Hebrew boy and calls him Moses, a name that joins both Egyptian and Israelite worlds. God has worked intimately in the hearts of women to save a Hebrew boy from the hand of evil. God brings to safety the beloved son who will deliver His people.

We see God provides, not in a grand spectacle but through intimately working in His people's hearts. He changes us to desire His will and to love the things He does. Through our faith in Jesus, we are involved in His redemptive mission to restore the world to His glory. Even when it seems God is not responding to our prayers, we can be confident that He is working in the smallest ways which will eventually have the greatest impact.

DESPITE HIS EFFORTS FOR CONTROL, PHARAOH DOES NOT HAVE POWER OVER GOD'S CHOSEN.

How does God begin to reveal His plan to save the Israelites?

_____

_____

_____

_____

_____

_____

_____

In what ways do the women reflect God's care for His beloved children?

_____

_____

_____

_____

_____

_____

_____

How do you react when God is silent?

_____

_____

_____

_____

_____

_____

_____

"EVEN IN TIMES OF DESPAIR, GOD IS COMMITTED TO HIS WORD AND IS WORKING TO REDEEM."

WEEK 1 / DAY 4

Fleeing from Duty

As an adopted prince of Egypt, Moses is raised in Pharaoh's court and grows in wealth and status. Moses is educated in the wisdom of Egyptian culture, and he becomes a promising leader with power and skill in oration and performance (Acts 7:22). Though royalty, he remains loyal to his true people, the Israelites. One day, he leaves the palace and goes out to be among the Hebrew slaves. Likely looking at their pain with empathy and with resolve to free them from the harsh labor, Moses assumes the people will know that God is going to use him to deliver them; however, this idea of Moses delivering them is something they do not yet understand (Acts 7:25). His God-given desire for justice is mixed with presumption. While Moses was visiting the Israelites, he witnessed an Egyptian beating an Israelite. The Scripture emphasizes this individual is "one of his people" (Exodus 2:11). Perhaps the blow to the Israelite slave is like a blow to Moses himself, he too feeling the sting of the Egyptian's whip. Moses is overcome with passion and rage. Neglecting to help the wounded slave, he calculates vengeance. Looking around and seeing no witnesses, he "struck the Egyptian dead" (Exodus 2:12). In an effort to hide what he has done, Moses then hides the man in the sand.

Despite Moses's failed work of deliverance, God does not leave Moses to his pride. Moses goes out again the following day, and he sees two Hebrews fighting. Attempting to judge the situation, Moses asks the aggressor, "Why are you attacking your neighbor?" (Exodus 2:13). The man rejects his counsel and exposes the murder Moses committed. He reveals the unrepentant sin in Moses's heart and confronts his injustice, making Moses unqualified to assume any type of moral authority. Moses retreats in fear. Could they have seen him? Did they find the body? Soon, word of Moses's deed spreads, and Pharaoh seeks to kill him. His Egyptian family has turned on him. The deliverer flees; Moses runs from his responsibility, deserts his people, and wanders alone in the land of Midian. He traverses the parched land. Finally, God brings Moses to a well in the land of Midian.

Now a fugitive, Moses finds a place to sit down at this well. Despite Moses's unjust act, God shows him mercy by providing refuge. Seven daughters of the priest of Midian appear. They are shepherdesses, drawing water for their father's sheep. Water supply is a highly sought-after commodity in the desert, and unfortunately, there are also shepherds present. The men drive the girls away. As in the events in Egypt, Moses sees injustice and chooses to step in and act. This time, he is not consumed with rage. Instead, he uses his God-given desire for righteousness appropriately. He saves the daughters, not by attacking the shepherds but by protecting the girls from them. Recognizing that he is not the perfect savior, Moses appears to have learned restraint. He does not have the authority to take justice into his own hands and afflict harm on evildoers. Instead, he turns his attention to the vulnerable and cares for the weak.

Perhaps astounded by Moses's actions, the daughters return to their home to tell their father of the Egyptian who rescued them and even drew water for their sheep. The priest asks his daughters to invite Moses to dinner and to stay with the family. Moses agrees and later marries the priest's daughter, Zipporah. The lost son is adopted again, now into a nomadic clan in the wilderness. Still, Moses feels out of place there, as expressed in the naming of his son, Gershom, for Moses explains, "I have been a resident alien in a foreign land" (Exodus 2:22). It is possible that Moses wrestles with a wavering identity: Hebrew by birth, Egyptian by class,

and Midianite by marriage. If so, he likely feels even more foreign, identifying with his people, the Israelites, when they first arrived in Goshen—though they were grateful to the Lord for saving them, what it must have been like to be in a new land! But through this role as a father, Moses has the opportunity to begin developing the servant-leadership needed for the future mission God has in store for him.

In preparing Moses, God does not forget His people. He hears the groans and cries for help in Egypt. He sees their affliction and grieves. Exodus 2:24-25 states, "God heard their groaning; and God remembered...God saw the Israelites, and God knew." God has not forgotten His people. Moses is emphasizing God's faithfulness. Even in times of despair, God is committed to His word and is working to redeem.

Though we might be placed in positions of power and influence, our efforts for good are in vain if they are not submitted to God's will. Without God at the center of our work, we are prone to depend on ourselves, unable to carry the weight of our expectations. Jesus alone can carry this responsibility to perfection. When we are lost in our failures, we can look to Him to give us our identity as His children and the proper foundation for redemptive work.

DESPITE MOSES'S FAILED WORK OF DELIVERANCE, GOD DOES NOT LEAVE MOSES TO HIS PRIDE BUT LEADS HIM OUT AGAIN.

What does Moses's failed act of deliverance reveal about the theology of salvation by grace?

How does God show mercy and faithfulness to Moses?

How do you respond when you see injustice?

"FULLY GOD, HE BECOMES A BABY, THE CHILD-KING DESERVING OF ALL PRAISE."

WEEK 1 / DAY 5

A Child Worthy of Worship

The events surrounding the birth of Moses highlight themes that are mirrored in the birth of Jesus. Matthew, one of the disciples, records His early years to characterize Jesus as the new Moses, sent to free God's chosen people from bondage. Though the Jewish nation is now under oppression from the Roman government, the real taskmaster is sin. Jesus has come to set His people free from spiritual slavery and leads them into God's rest and presence.

Like Moses, Jesus begins His mission as a baby. But unlike Moses, the eternal Son of God, Jesus, takes on human flesh. Fully God, He becomes a baby, the child-king deserving of all praise. This is a birth etched in eternity, a plan rooted in the foreknowledge of God. As Mary labors through the pains, the whole earth is expectant of the new life to come. Studying the earth's signs and Old Testament prophecy, wise men from the east travel to Jerusalem to meet the Messiah who has been born. There, they inquire about his whereabouts to Herod the Great, Rome's King of Judea. Like Pharaoh, Herod is paranoid about a loss of power and is threatened by this new King. Herod is also deceptive. As an agent of evil, he secretly seeks to destroy the promised Son of God who will establish His sovereign authority and good kingdom.

The wise men follow the star to a place in Bethlehem and finally witness the beloved Son. When the wise men see the child with his mother they rejoice and bow down in worship. They bestow Jesus with the finest incense and the most beautiful treasures. His birth cannot be hidden. A host of angels reveals the news to shepherds (Luke 2:8-14), and all come to admire him. Both human and spiritual beings recognize this birth as unlike any that has ever before occurred. His name is Immanuel, which means, "God with us."

Herod begins his search for the boy. The angel of the Lord comes to Joseph, Mary's husband, in a dream and tells him to take the child and his mother to Egypt to escape Herod's grip (Matthew 2:13-14). Matthew does not refer to Jesus as Joseph's son in this verse. Despite knowing Jesus is not his biological child, Joseph adopts the boy and still seeks His protection. So he immediately gets up and obeys the instructions. Similar to Moses, Jesus has the identity of an adopted son who is of two worlds. But, Jesus's worlds are both human and divine. He has to navigate His time on earth as a foreigner, whose home is in heaven.

Seeking refuge in Egypt, Jesus stays there while Herod kills all the male children in Bethlehem. Once again, Satan tries to destroy the seed of the woman but fails. Satan is closer to his defeat. The cries of Jewish women pour out over the land, mirroring the Israelite women in Egypt when their sons were thrown into the Nile River. Matthew uses Old Testament prophecies from Jeremiah 31:15 that describe the sorrowful women of Judah whose sons had been captured and killed in the Babylonian exile. In the next section of Jeremiah 31, God promises the exiled Israelites will come back from the land of the enemy and return to their own country (Jeremiah 31:16-17). God calls the exiled nation His "precious son" (Jeremiah 31:20) whom He will remember and protect. Matthew applies this text to comfort the women in Bethlehem and all who have been oppressed by evil. The beloved Son has been kept from harm and will return to Judea to complete His mission.

After Herod's death, the angel of the Lord tells Joseph it is now safe to take the child and his mother to the land of Israel. They leave Egypt, fulfilling the words of the prophet Hosea that state, "When Israel was a child, I loved him, and out of Egypt I called my son" (Hosea 11:1). His family settles in Nazareth.

Moses's birth foreshadowed the birth of Jesus, the promised Redeemer. Jesus is the Messiah who was predicted in Genesis 3:15. Genesis 3:15 prophesied the seed of the woman who would defeat spiritual evil and accomplish the work of salvation. This verse finds its fulfillment in the birth of Mary's son, Jesus. He came as the Anointed One to establish God's kingdom and free us from sin. But, He came and lived first as a baby wrapped in swaddling cloth. Jesus was born for us and God's glory. We should look at His birth as no mundane event but as a miracle. God loved us so much that He sent His Son to enter the world in vulnerability and kept Him from harm until His death on the cross. But, even after that day, God raised His precious Son from the grave and bestowed on Him all honor and glory. We should remember that the gospel starts with a birth, and that should cause us to live with thankfulness for His coming.

SIMILAR TO MOSES, JESUS HAS THE IDENTITY OF AN ADOPTED SON WHO IS OF TWO WORLDS. BUT, JESUS'S WORLDS ARE BOTH HUMAN AND DIVINE.

What are some similarities and differences between the birth of Moses and the birth of Jesus?

BIRTH OF MOSES	BIRTH OF JESUS

Read John 1:14. What is the significance of God becoming human in the person of Jesus?

_____

_____

_____

_____

_____

_____

How does the birth of the precious Son provide you hope and comfort?

_____

_____

_____

_____

_____

_____

_____

SIN HAS MY HEART BOUND WITH LARGE METAL CHAINS
PULLING MY DESIRES TOWARD REBELLION
A CRUEL TASKMASTER, SIN IS NOT ASHAMED
WHEN IT STRIKES THE WORD OF GOD, TRANSGRESSION

CAPTIVE, I AM FORCED TO WORK TO NO END
BUILDING STRUCTURES FOR MAN'S PRIDE AND GLORY
SERVING LEECHES WHO CLAIM GODS; THEY PRETEND
LEAVING ME WEAK, MALNOURISHED IN BODY

MY CRIES CALL FOR THE DELIVERER SENT
TO BREAK THE SHACKLES OF SIN AND EVIL
TO RESTORE LIFE AND A FUTURE CONTENT
THIS ONE, JESUS, WILL RESCUE HIS PEOPLE

Kyra Daniels

JESUS RESPONDED,
"TRULY I TELL YOU,
EVERYONE WHO
COMMITS SIN IS
A SLAVE OF SIN."

John 8:34

Week 01 Reflection

Summarize the main points from this week's Scripture readings.

_____

_____

_____

_____

_____

_____

_____

_____

_____

_____

_____

_____

What did you observe from this week's passages about God and His character?

_____

_____

_____

_____

_____

_____

_____

_____

_____

_____

_____

What do this week's passages reveal about the condition of mankind and yourself?

_____

_____

_____

_____

_____

_____

_____

_____

How do these passages point to the gospel?

_____

_____

_____

_____

_____

How should you respond to these Scriptures? What specific action steps can you take this week to apply them in your life?

_____

_____

_____

_____

_____

_____

_____

_____

Write a prayer in response to your study of God's Word. Adore God for who He is, confess sins that He revealed in your own life, ask Him to empower you to walk in obedience, and pray for anyone who comes to mind as you study.

_____

_____

_____

_____

_____

_____

_____

God Sees His Sheep

"EVEN THOUGH HE DOES NOT SEE GOD'S HAND, MOSES IS BEING GUIDED BY THE GOOD SHEPHERD."

WEEK 2 / DAY 1

Moses Meets the Shepherd

Forty years pass, and Moses is now a shepherd of his father-in-law's herd of sheep. At eighty years old, he has a different identity and way of life than when he was a prince in Egypt. He has taken the humble role of a servant, patiently leading sheep across the wilderness. God is using the menial task to prepare him for a great mission. He learns the temperaments of the sheep: dependent, fearful, and defenseless. In this role, he also gains an understanding of the geographic layout. Developing probable skills of servant-leadership and spatial awareness will be important in the next phase of his journey. One day, Moses sets off to Mount Horeb, also known as Mount Sinai, bringing the sheep to an uncultivated area in the region. In His providence, God leads Moses here. Even though he does not see God's hand, Moses is being guided by the Good Shepherd. In the distance, Moses sees a remarkable sight of fire burning within a bush. The angel of the Lord comes to him in this miracle. This phenomenon is called a theophany, a visible manifestation of the invisible God. Most scholars agree that the angel of the Lord is the pre-incarnate Jesus, the Son of God sent as a divine messenger before taking the form of a man. God's sustaining control, brilliance, and independent power are on display in this theophany.

The mystery of God draws Moses. God calls his name. Before Moses realizes the author of this miracle, God already knows him intimately. Moses recognizes the voice of God and responds, "Here I am." Recognizing His lordship, God's chosen people are His sheep; they answer and flock to Him when called. God stops Moses and warns him not to come any closer to the flame. This command is gracious, letting Moses know that the presence of God cannot be approached casually. God's glory would have consumed Moses if he had approached it irreverently. God tells Moses to remove his sandals to protect the holiness of the place. Through the directive, God is teaching that His space cannot be defiled. Moses is standing on holy ground, set apart from the rest of the world.

God initiates this encounter and introduces Himself as the God of the Hebrews. He personalizes His relationship to the Israelite nation through Moses's father. Moses had lived most of his life without his real father and likely unsure of his identity. God reminds Moses who he is: a Hebrew man from the tribe of Levi. God continues to proclaim He is the covenant God of the patriarchs—Abraham, Isaac, and Jacob. God has promised they would be a great nation, possess the land of Canaan, be a blessing to other nations, and forever live in His presence. Living with the priest of Midian as His father-in-law, Moses must have known about God's covenant with the Israelite patriarch, Abraham, in Genesis 12:1-3. Now it is no longer a distant promise, however, but a present reality. As he realizes the glorious God before him, Moses hides his face in the fear of the Lord. He is full of respect and awe at being known by the God of the universe.

God has seen the torment of slavery on His people in Egypt and has heard their prayers for relief. He has grieved with them in their suffering, and now, God has come to rescue them from bondage. The covenant relationship between God and the Israelites deepens to reveal a saving component. Salvation will be a work of God based on the commitment to His word and His affections for His people. He will bring them from bitterness to rejoicing. He will lead them to the land of Canaan, "a good and spacious land, a land flowing with milk and honey" (Exodus 3:8). God will bless with abundance and plenty after years of lack. He will dispossess the pagan nations such as the Canaanites, Hittites, Amorites, Perizzites, Hivites, and Jebusites. Though they have corrupted the land, He will establish His holiness there.

God incorporates Moses into His plan of salvation. Though freedom will be the result of God's divine action, God involves human obedience. He commands Moses to go to Pharaoh and lead His people out of Egypt.

In today's passage, we see that salvation starts with God alone. His work initiates, sustains, and achieves the plan to save us from sin. We cannot save ourselves from our rebellious hearts or from captivity to spiritual evil. First in His act of salvation is condescension, meaning God Himself stoops down to our level and abides among us. We see this in the person of Jesus Christ. God came down and took the form of a man to reveal the freeing love of the Father. We can rest in God's abiding presence in Jesus and trust in His saving work.

HE HAS GRIEVED WITH THEM IN THEIR SUFFERING, AND NOW, GOD HAS COME TO RESCUE THEM FROM BONDAGE.

How does God shepherd Moses?

_____
_____
_____
_____
_____
_____
_____
_____
_____

What does God reveal about His character through the theophany in this passage?

_____
_____
_____
_____
_____
_____
_____
_____
_____

How has God freed you from sin and brought you into His abundance?

_____
_____
_____
_____
_____
_____
_____
_____
_____

"THE GREAT I AM
HAS DESCENDED
FROM HIS
HEAVENLY THRONE
TO FREE THEM."

WEEK 2 / DAY 2

READ EXODUS 3:11-4:17

Directed by the Great I AM

It seems that Moses's insecurities paralyze him. He cannot confront Pharaoh and lead God's people out of Egypt. But when Moses questions God, He redirects his attention to divine sufficiency. Comforting him, God says He will certainly be with Moses and will bring the Israelites to this mountain. Here, they will be free to worship God, no longer servants to Pharaoh and his idol statues. But Moses's questioning continues as he seemingly fears the opinions of men. What if the Israelites are skeptical? What if they have forgotten? God reveals Himself as "I AM WHO I AM," His eternal name (Exodus 3:14). The name, I AM, encompasses the attributes of God. God does not change. His power is everlasting. He is self-sufficient, self-existing, and self-sustaining. The great I AM is unlike any god the Israelites have encountered in Egypt, and He has descended from His heavenly throne to free them.

God then gives Moses the role of prophet. He is to proclaim the words of the Lord to the elders. The elders are representatives from the twelve tribes of Jacob. Through Moses, God will reestablish His relationship with the sons of Israel. These men have seen slavery year after year, but God has seen their anguish and will fulfill His will. Now is the time for elders to restore their faith and return to the Promised Land. God assures Moses they will heed his message and stand in solidarity with him. Moses is to ask Pharaoh to let the Hebrew slaves go on a three-day journey to worship in the wilderness. The Israelites cannot rightly worship the Holy God in an idol-corrupted land like Egypt.

God foreknows that even a kind tone and a small request will not soften Pharaoh's heart—he will not give permission. Pharaoh will likely fear a loss of control and be offended by the Israelites' religious defiance. As a result, stubborn and hardened, he will keep a firm grasp on the slaves, so a battle will commence. God will then stretch out His hand, striking Egypt, and will perform powerful and wondrous miracles in the sight of Pharaoh, pressuring him to release the Israelites. They will leave, receiving gold and silver from the Egyptians, fulfilling the promise to Abraham in Genesis

15:14. The Israelites will march out like a victorious army, adorned with the spoils of war.

Moses wrestles with the wrong outcomes that are possible. But, God uses this third rebuttal to showcase His might. God has Moses recognize the object in his hand—a staff. This a simple, shepherd's tool to prod sheep. He tells Moses to throw it on the ground, and Moses does. The staff transforms into a snake, and Moses runs away afraid. Poisonous snakes are a dangerous threat to wilderness travelers like shepherds, but God shows Moses that with Him, what appears deadly is nothing to fear. Using similar language from Exodus 3:20, the Lord directs Moses to stretch out his hand and pick up the slithering creature by its tail. This method is most dangerous because the snake's mouth is open to bite. Incredibly, in Moses's hand, the snake turns back into a staff. God will use Moses to show His supernatural authority over the created realm. Additionally, He performs a second sign. At the Lord's command, Moses places his hand inside his cloak and takes it out to see it has been stricken with the disease, leprosy. It would be no surprise for Moses to stare in horror at the peeling and lifeless skin. God tells him to repeat the action, and when he removes his hand from his clothing again, the flesh is restored to health. The Egyptians have sought help from their idols to beat leprosy, but God shows He is the Lord with extraordinary ability to overcome a ravaging disease. Finally, God gives Moses a third sign of turning water into blood, but not even Moses himself is convinced.

For the fourth time, Moses offers another excuse. He claims to be inarticulate, having lost the oratory skill he had as a prince. The Lord, who is slow to anger, has patiently given Moses reason to trust Him, but He ultimately will not tolerate the questioning of His authority and judgment. When Moses asks God to send someone else, His anger erupts from the burning bush. God is the maker of all, and He can equip Moses in his slow speech. Moses cannot flee from his duty again. God has already called for his brother Aaron to serve as a prophet in his place, but Moses will continue as the deliverer, showing the power of God through his shepherd's staff.

Today, we see that God makes His power known through human weakness. Our insecurities and inabilities are no challenge to God's plans. He will still involve us in His divine action to show that He is our ultimate source of strength and ability. We should not evade responsibility out of fear and doubt of His authority but rather, depend on His Spirit through faith in Jesus to empower and equip us for His glory.

MOSES WILL CONTINUE AS THE DELIVERER, SHOWING THE POWER OF GOD THROUGH HIS SHEPHERD'S STAFF.

Which of God's attributes are significant in your life?

☐ Eternal	☐ Good	☐ Gracious	☐ Holy
☐ Immanent	☐ Immutable	☐ Just	☐ Love
☐ Merciful	☐ Omnipotent	☐ Omnipresent	☐ Omniscient
☐ Righteous	☐ Self-existent	☐ Sovereign	☐ Transcendent

How do the written miracles of God in Scripture impact your faith?

_____

_____

_____

_____

_____

_____

_____

_____

Describe a time when God used your weaknesses for His glory.

_____

_____

_____

_____

_____

_____

_____

_____

"EVEN THOUGH MOSES IS THE CHOSEN DELIVERER, HE IS A FALLEN HUMAN BEING."

WEEK 2 / DAY 3

Failing the Firstborn

God calls Moses back to Egypt to free the Israelites from slavery, though he feels hesitant. Realizing he cannot evade this task, Moses accepts. He returns to his father-in-law's place in Midian to ask for permission to leave. Jethro permits him and blesses his travel. Without even knowing the actual details of his trip, the priest of Midian speaks words of encouragement to Moses's worried heart. Before he sets off, the Lord identifies the reason for his hesitation. Moses still feels marked by his past. God assures him that he will be safe to return to Egypt as the men who wanted to harm him are dead. Moses trusts God's word and responds in obedience. He puts his wife and two sons, Gershom and Eliezer, on a donkey and heads for the land of Egypt, staff in hand. Now, this staff belongs to God. Through it, God will demonstrate His might and wonder. The staff itself is not magical, but it is a sign of the divine authority Moses is given. Pharaoh will witness the miracles of the one true God, but instead of being moved to believe, he will remain stubborn. God will give Pharaoh over to his rebellious desires, but his obduracy will lead to a greater manifestation of God's glory.

The Lord calls the nation His firstborn son, for whom He will go to unimaginable lengths so that they can worship Him freely. Pharaoh will repay the wrongs committed against God's son and experience a punishment equal to His oppression. Pharaoh will feel grief as God did when seeing the Israelites put in captivity and to death. His unyielding attitude will offer up his own firstborn son to be taken by the judgment and wrath of God.

While Moses and his family are staying at an overnight campsite in the wilderness, resting from their travels, the Lord comes to Moses in righteous anger. Scholars differ on the details of this scene, but this passage is most often interpreted as God confronting Moses about his neglecting to circumcise his firstborn son, Gershom. In Genesis 17:9-14, when God instituted His covenant with Abraham, He defined circumcision as the outward symbol of faithful obedience. Circumcision would set the Israelites apart as God's chosen people and would demonstrate that the Israelites are committed to serving Him. Moses, thinking circumcision an insignificant act, disobeys an essential condition of the Lord's covenant, seemingly showing a lack of faithfulness, and, therefore, puts his life at risk. Even though Moses is the chosen deliverer, he is a fallen human being, and it is in God's character to express justice toward all rebellion. Moses's wife, Zipporah, acts quickly and grabs a flint knife to circumcise their son herself. Zipporah intervenes where Moses fails. To save her husband from his due punishment, in haste, Zipporah throws the blood from the cut skin at his feet. Zipporah understands the shedding of the firstborn's blood covers sin and clears the debt of disobedience. Then, the Lord relents from His anger and is merciful. Again, Moses is saved by the Spirit of God working within a woman. But, this time, her actions are the result of his negligence. Perhaps because his poor leadership created possible distance and disappointment in their relationship, Moses sends her and their sons back to their home in Midian (Exodus 18:2-4).

Now, Moses continues his journey alone. He comes to Mount Horeb where God first met with him in the burning bush. He remembers the promises and signs the Lord showed him. In the distance, Moses spots a man approaching. Moses does not recognize the person and fears for his life again. But, the man comes to him in gentle amazement. He reveals himself as Aaron, Moses's brother, directed by God to meet with him in the wilderness. Moses is likely full of joy at this reunion. Finally, he has reconnected with one like him. Feeling the kinship bond, Moses tells Aaron all that God told and showed him on the mountain. In His grace, God provides Aaron as a companion and help. They finish their journey, arriving in the land of Goshen to meet with the elders. Aaron relays the information from Moses and performs the signs. Immediately, people believe and are relieved that God has answered their prayers. Instead of the skepticism Moses feared, the people worship.

In today's passage, we see the theme of God's love toward His firstborn son. The nation of Israel was a type of Christ. This phrase means that Israel was a picture of the coming of Jesus. Israel was the imperfect son who would end up rebelling against God. But, Jesus is the perfect firstborn Son of God who is obedient to the Father. In this love, God did not leave Jesus to death but raised Him to life, honor, and glory. Additionally, God loves us, His chosen sons and daughters, through the sacrifice of His firstborn Son. In love, Jesus covered our sins with His blood. We escape the wrath of God and become His beloved children, inheriting the promise of the covenant and reward of Jesus's faithfulness.

THE SHEDDING OF THE FIRSTBORN'S BLOOD COVERS SIN AND CLEARS THE DEBT OF DISOBEDIENCE.

What qualities of God's character are revealed during the scene at the campsite?

_____

_____

_____

_____

_____

_____

_____

Was circumcision a prerequisite for the covenant with God or a result of it?

_____

_____

_____

_____

_____

_____

_____

Are there sins in your life that need to be covered by the blood of the firstborn?

_____

_____

_____

_____

_____

_____

_____

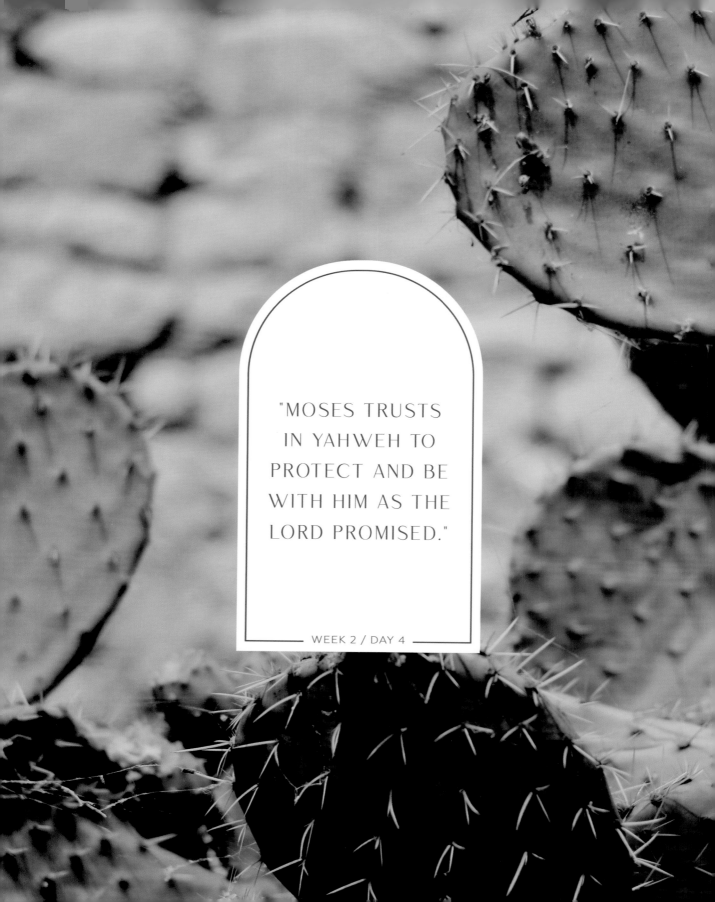

"MOSES TRUSTS IN YAHWEH TO PROTECT AND BE WITH HIM AS THE LORD PROMISED."

WEEK 2 / DAY 4

Confronting the Past

Moses and Aaron enter the Egyptian palace, the place that was once his home forty years ago. But Moses faces his past with courage. He has met the true and living God whose glory surpasses all the pompous display of Egypt. Moses trusts in Yahweh to protect and be with him as the Lord promised. Moses and Aaron stand in front of Pharaoh and relay the Lord's demand for the Israelites to be released from labor so that they can have a festival for Him in the wilderness. Scholars argue this request is nothing out of the ordinary, as historical evidence shows that pharaohs at times would give their slaves time off to worship their gods. But, this pharaoh responds in ignorance and skepticism.

Moses and Aaron specify it is the God of the Hebrew slaves who has made this demand, and He will punish Egypt if Pharaoh is resistant. Pharaoh dismisses Moses and Aaron and blames them for getting in the way of the people's productivity. Behind Pharaoh's accusation is his belief that the identity and the value of the Israelites are only found in service to him. He places on their shoulders the weight of working for their worth. He denies seeing them as people chosen to live freely in worship of God. Emboldened from his authority being challenged, Pharaoh demands the taskmasters to make the slave labor more difficult by not providing straw for brickmaking. Pharaoh then calls the Lord's words deceptive (Exodus 5:9). Like the serpent in the garden of Eden, Pharaoh asserts the God of the Hebrews is the malevolent one. But, in reality, he is distracting the Israelites from the goodness of God with his oppressive work. The taskmasters beat the Israelites when they do not provide the same number of bricks as they did when straw was provided. The Israelites come to Pharaoh for some relief, but he does not save them from the taskmasters' beatings. Callous to their burdens and worsening the abuse, Pharaoh berates them and calls them slackers. Service to evil is shameful. The Israelites are viewed as worthless and irresponsible when they do not measure up to Pharaoh's productivity standards.

Moses and Aaron see this situation does not look good. In addition to Pharaoh's resistance, now they have lost the Israelites' support. In the people's eyes, Moses and Aaron have gone from deliverers to destroyers. This failure at the start of their mission is not what Moses expected. He had obeyed the Lord's command to leave the comfort of shepherding and return to Egypt. He trusted in God to free the Israelites, but this harsher labor is not freedom. Moses goes to God and asks, "Lord, why have you caused trouble for this people? And why did you ever send me? Ever since I went in to Pharaoh to speak in your name he has caused trouble for this people, and you haven't rescued your people at all" (Exodus 5:22-23). It seems that Moses's fear and failure cause him to blame God and regret being sent to Egypt. But, scholars argue that his going to God in his time of trouble shows relational growth. Moses has discovered more about God since meeting with Him on the mountain. Instead of simply bailing on the mission, Moses goes to God with his concerns and questions, knowing the Lord can provide the answers.

God will reveal His power through Pharaoh's resistance. Though now Pharaoh is resistant to even a small request like a three-day journey, God assures Moses that by the Lord's strong hand, Pharaoh will drive the slaves out of Egypt for good. Despite the unsettling confrontation, Yahweh is still in control. His sovereign plans are unfolding, and He does not operate on human schedules. Though the situation seems bleak to Moses now, from the Lord's perspective, this incident is no setback. The mission is not finished. Rather, the initial failure is included in the Lord's divine will to show how God will move an extremely stubborn oppressor to act for the Israelites' redemption. The Lord then recites His covenant promises and gives commands for Moses and Aaron to approach Pharaoh again; it is time for God's power to be on full display.

In today's passage, we see that Moses ultimately rested in God's righteousness to rescue the people instead of taking matters into his own hands like he did when he was a prince. Though back in Egypt, Moses had changed. He did not rely on himself but sought help from God. The Israelites did not yet know this type of rest, as they had to endlessly work to be in good standing with Pharaoh. Their work is a picture of the righteousness we try to earn for ourselves outside the rest of Jesus. Through the saving work of Jesus, our Savior frees us from condemnation and shame when we fail. His righteousness won for us rest in God's presence. Therefore, we can be patient when God acts more slowly than we want or in ways we do not expect. It is not up to us; the Lord will accomplish His good and perfect will in our lives.

IT IS TIME FOR GOD'S POWER TO BE ON FULL DISPLAY.

Describe times when you are caught up in stressful or burdensome productivity. What physical, mental, and emotional impact does this have on you?

_____

_____

_____

_____

_____

_____

_____

_____

What or whom are you motivated to serve during these times?

_____

_____

_____

_____

_____

_____

How do you handle failure? Write a prayer to God, asking Him to give you rest and patience in these moments.

_____

_____

_____

_____

_____

_____

_____

"JESUS IS
THE WAY TO
BE SAVED."

WEEK 2 / DAY 5

The Good Shepherd

The role of shepherd is a theme that connects Moses and Jesus. In Midian, Moses protected and cared for his sheep as he saw they were helpless and vulnerable without his provision. He would do the same for the people of Israel when leading them out of Egypt. This account exposes a human need for a shepherd and points to true guidance in Jesus. In the Matthew and John passages, Jesus declares He is the Good Shepherd who will protect His sheep and lead them to life.

In Matthew 9:35-36, Jesus carries out His ministry in the region of Galilee. He goes to various places to heal people from sickness and to proclaim the good news of God's kingdom. Through His healing, Jesus is breaking the curse in Genesis 3 where Adam and Eve disobeyed God's command not to eat of the Tree of Knowledge of Good and Evil. As a result of their actions, sin entered the world and polluted humanity. The curse of death has led not only to moral corruption but also to erosion and weakening of the body. The people of Galilee are burdened by the effects of sin and are desperate for restoration. They hear about Jesus's miracles and draw to the presence of their Savior. When the crowds surround Him, Jesus looks at them with compassion. He sees their downcast state and identifies them as "sheep without a shepherd" (Matthew 9:36). Jesus also calls them to repentance, forgives their sins, and points them to the kingdom of God, a spiritual establishment of God's authority on earth. Though they battle bodily weaknesses, they can be spiritually whole through restoration found in Him. He heals the people as a sign of the eternal life they will have in His kingdom and a manifestation of His power as the true Shepherd.

Jesus reveals Himself as the Good Shepherd when He is in Jerusalem and travels from Galilee to Judea to declare His lordship at the center place of worship. There, He heals a man who was born blind and, most importantly, gives him eyes to see that Jesus is the Messiah. Jesus is then met with suspicion and criticism from the Pharisees, the leading religious teachers who held strict observance of the law. Though the Pharisees are knowledgeable of the Scriptures, they are spiritually blinded by their hypocrisy and superiority. They do not recognize the prophesied Savior who has now come before them.

In John 10:1-18, Jesus responds to their questioning with a description involving sheep, a sheep pen, a shepherd, and a thief. He identifies the thief as one who does not enter through the sheep pen's gate but climbs over it. The thief is not permitted by the gatekeeper to enter, so he tries to do so cunningly. But, the gatekeeper opens the gate for the shepherd exclusively. Inside, the shepherd calls the name of his sheep, and they respond to His voice alone. After the people did not understand this narrative, Jesus follows with indicative "I Am" statements, declaring upon Himself the eternal name of God that was first spoken to Moses in Exodus 3:14. He says, "I am the gate for the sheep." Jesus is the way to be saved. Those in Him can "come in and go out" with freedom, knowing they are protected by the gate structure. Having this security, the sheep who are the people of God will have life and rest. But, the wicked leaders and agents of spiritual evil are thieves who attempt to bring the people of God under their control. Jesus not only declares to be the way to life — He then says, "I am the good shepherd." He is the one who guides His sheep, sacrifices His life for them, and will not abandon them to wolves. Jesus then says, "I know my sheep, and my own know me." The word "know" indicates an intimate relationship between Jesus and His people. Their union reflects the bond between Jesus and God the Father. Lastly, Jesus emphasizes His mission to bring all His sheep into one flock, and through accomplishing His Father's will, He will be a shepherd over them. He will gather all believers, both Jews and Gentiles, and they will worship the Lord together as His church.

In today's passages, we see that God uses a man with shepherd-like qualities to carry out His redemptive mission. God first showed this with Moses. While shepherding Jethro's flock for forty years, Moses gained leadership, patience, and gentle care needed to shepherd the Israelites. But Jesus possesses these qualities perfectly. As the eternal Son of God, He is the Good Shepherd who not only cares for but also rescues His lost sheep. Through the gospel, we understand we have been taken captive by thieves and are vulnerable to wolves. In this world, we are subject to abuse, deceived by lies, and can lose our God-given identity to societal standards. But, Jesus saves, secures, and sustains us on our walk with Him. We should realize that we are His sheep and stay near to His staff, depending on Him for guidance and protection.

JESUS IS THE ONE WHO GUIDES HIS SHEEP, SACRIFICES HIS LIFE FOR THEM, AND WILL NOT ABANDON THEM TO WOLVES.

Identify and describe someone you know with shepherd-like qualities.

_____

_____

_____

_____

_____

_____

_____

_____

How is Jesus the true and better Shepherd?

_____

_____

_____

_____

_____

_____

_____

_____

As a sheep under Jesus's covering, how should you navigate life?

_____

_____

_____

_____

_____

_____

_____

LISTEN TO THE HYMN, "COME, THOU FOUNT OF EVERY BLESSING," AND MEDITATE ON THE LYRICS BELOW.

OH, TO GRACE HOW GREAT A DEBTOR
DAILY I'M CONSTRAINED TO BE
LET THAT GOODNESS LIKE A FETTER
BIND MY WANDERING HEART TO THEE
PRONE TO WANDER, LORD, I FEEL IT
PRONE TO LEAVE THE GOD I LOVE
HERE'S MY HEART, OH, TAKE AND SEAL IT
SEAL IT FOR THY COURTS ABOVE

Robert Robinson
"Come, Thou Fount of Every Blessing"
1758

I AM THE GOOD
SHEPHERD. THE GOOD
SHEPHERD LAYS DOWN HIS
LIFE FOR THE SHEEP.

John 10:11

Week 02 Reflection

Summarize the main points from this week's Scripture readings.

_____

_____

_____

_____

_____

_____

_____

_____

_____

_____

_____

_____

What did you observe from this week's passages about God and His character?

_____

_____

_____

_____

_____

_____

_____

_____

_____

_____

_____

_____

What do this week's passages reveal about the condition of mankind and yourself?

_____

_____

_____

_____

_____

_____

_____

How do these passages point to the gospel?

How should you respond to these Scriptures? What specific action steps can you take this week to apply them in your life?

Write a prayer in response to your study of God's Word. Adore God for who He is, confess sins that He revealed in your own life, ask Him to empower you to walk in obedience, and pray for anyone who comes to mind as you study.

The Deliverer Who Sings

WEEK THREE

"THEY ENLIST INTO THE ARMY OF GOD AND BENEFIT FROM HIS SOLE VICTORY OVER THE EGYPTIANS."

WEEK 3 / DAY 1

In the Lord's Army

Though already making His mission and character clear to Moses, God is patient with him. He knows Moses is threatened by the opinions of men, and when his first task to Pharaoh is a flop, God comes to Moses graciously and enables him to trust. The Lord tells Moses He will bring the Israelites out of Egypt in military divisions, resembling an army in battle.

Moses and Aaron approach Pharaoh's throne again. As the Lord commanded, Aaron throws down his staff, and it transforms into a serpent at their feet. As snake worshipers, Pharaoh and his officials are challenged by their deity's subordination to the Israelite men. So Pharaoh calls the court magicians to face off against his opponent. Using forces of spiritual evil, they also turn their staffs into serpents. God's supernatural power is met with the sorcery of Egypt's occult practitioners. But they are no match for God Almighty. The serpent of Moses and Aaron swallows the serpents of the magicians and turns back into a staff in Aaron's hand. Pharaoh looks at them, unmoved by their superior power. His reaction confirms his hard heart and launches Egypt into a battle with the Lord.

By the staff of Moses and Aaron, God unleashes a series of strikes against Pharaoh. They are described as the ten plagues in Scripture. Each one delivers an attack on the deities of Egypt, showing the ultimate power of the God of the Israelites. Through this judgment, God also highlights His mercy and loving-kindness for the Israelites. All humans have sinned and fallen short of God's standard (Romans 3:23), so the Hebrew slaves possess the same rebellious hearts as the Egyptians. But, the Lord has chosen them to be His people and has kept them to be faithful for His good pleasure. By no action of their own have they merited this grace. They enlist into the army of God and benefit from His sole victory over the Egyptians.

The plagues occur in groups of three. The first two in each group begin with Moses and Aaron going to Pharaoh to request their departure and then giving a prophetic warning of the plague to come. The third plague in each group is inflicted without request or warning. This structure escalates, showing that the Lord is patient for Pharaoh's repentance. The plagues culminate in the tenth one which is the most severe — God will strike down every firstborn male in Egypt. After receiving the word from the Lord, Moses informs the Israelites to cover their doorposts with the blood of a young sheep or goat. The sacrificial offering will serve as a distinguishing mark protecting the Israelites from God's judgment upon the land of Egypt (Exodus 12:13). Moses tells them they are to remember this time as the holy day, Passover, when the Lord's wrath passed over them. Fulfilling His word in Exodus 4:23, God strikes down every firstborn male in Egypt at midnight, even Pharaoh's son. Wailing and screams of horror are heard throughout Egypt. But the Israelites are protected. In probable grief and distress, Pharaoh calls for Moses and Aaron and tells them to take the Israelites, with their possessions and flocks, and leave Egypt. Pharaoh's pride has finally been broken.

The Israelites quickly pack supplies and unleavened bread for the journey. The unrisen dough will also be consumed during Passover and the Festival of Unleavened Bread to commemorate this time of new life. Fearing another plague, the Egyptians give the slaves silver, gold, and clothing to appease Yahweh, the God of Israel. The Israelites depart in favor and fulfill the promise in Genesis 15:14. Like a triumphant army, the Israelites plunder Egypt. And like a commander of infantry, Moses leads the nation out of Egypt on foot into the dark landscape.

In today's reading, we see the character of God as a victor and protector. By His might, He judged Egypt's gods and its oppressive regime. By His mercy, He rescued the Israelites from slavery through the covering blood of the Passover Lamb. Moses becomes commander of the Lord's army, delivering God's people from the adversary's hand. Moses's leadership in this scene foreshadows the commander of heaven's army, Jesus. Through His faithfulness, Jesus has set captives free and has pronounced victory over spiritual evil. And, when He returns to establish His eternal kingdom, He will come prepared for war to do away with spiritual evil completely (Revelation 19:11-16). Jesus is also the true Passover Lamb. Just as the blood of a lamb covered the Israelites during the final plague, Jesus's sacrifice on the cross has covered us in God's love. His blood that was shed and His body that was broken satisfied God's justice and paid our debts. His death made it possible for us to escape slavery to sin and live as God's own. We are truly saved by the great commander and Passover Lamb, Jesus. Follow Him, for His glorious victory over evil has given us freedom and a new life. Stay under His care, for His merciful protection helps us know God's love and forgiveness.

LIKE A COMMANDER OF INFANTRY, MOSES LEADS THE NATION OUT OF EGYPT ON FOOT INTO THE DARK LANDSCAPE.

THE TEN PLAGUES

Water to Blood *Exodus 7:14-25*	Frogs *Exodus 8:1-15*	Gnats *Exodus 8:16-19*	Flies *Exodus 8:20-32*	Death of Livestock *Exodus 9:1-7*
Unhealing Boils *Exodus 9:8-12*	Hail *Exodus 9:13-35*	Locusts *Exodus 10:1-20*	Complete Darkness *Exodus 10:21-29*	Death of the First Born *Exodus 11:1–12:36*

How do Moses and Pharaoh both oppose God's authority? How does God's will of justice and mercy separate the result of their opposition?

_____

_____

_____

_____

In what way does the Lord's Supper, or Communion, help you to remember Jesus's victory and protection?

_____

_____

_____

_____

How do you react to knowing that Jesus has won your battle against sin?

_____

_____

_____

_____

"LIKE GOD'S ABIDING PRESENCE IN THE CLOUD AND FIRE, JESUS NEVER LEAVES US TO PURSUE HOLINESS BY OURSELVES."

WEEK 3 / DAY 2

Led by a Pillar of Cloud and Fire

A night of flight and death brings a morning of remembrance. Moses looks over the ex-slaves who now stand as a united people. Moses and the Israelites have witnessed miracles. They now know the Lord as the God who redeems and is faithful to fulfill His promises. After receiving the command, Moses gathers the people's attention and calls them to consecration. Consecration refers to an action to set apart a people or place to reflect the holiness of God. This concept is familiar to Moses as he witnessed the holiness of God on Mount Horeb in Exodus 3:5. There, the ground upon which he stood was consecrated for the Lord. With first-hand experience of the Lord's power, Moses has more confidence now to speak God's messages. He does not use Aaron as his mouthpiece but has learned to rely on divine ability. Moses tells them to consecrate themselves by commemorating Passover and dedicating all firstborn males to the Lord.

As seen in yesterday's passage, Passover and the Festival of Unleavened Bread are to be recognized among the Israelites as holy days symbolizing the beginning of new life. The people are to remember when God brought them out of slavery by His mighty power. Moses gives them the details for consecration. To point back to their immediate escape from slavery, no leavened bread will be eaten during this period. Moses informs them that this custom is to be passed down through the generations. They are to mark these instructions on their hands and foreheads. These actions will consecrate their bodies, keeping the Lord at the center of life and meditating on His commands daily.

Moses continues his speech with the consecration of the firstborn sons. Upon entering the Promised Land, all firstborn males are to be dedicated to the Lord. The firstborn of the animals are to be sacrificed as a substitutionary atonement, which means a replacement would receive the punishment for the injustices of humanity. God's law reveals that the shedding of blood is required for His forgiveness (Hebrews 9:22). As representatives, the firstborn males of their animal flock will be sacrificed to reconcile the people to the Father. This act will also cause the Israelites to remember the night of Passover when the blood of the sacrificial lamb covered them from God's judgment. Again, Moses tells the people to make a sign or symbol for this command on their hands and foreheads.

Moses steps into the role of leader. He follows the direction of the Lord as they head toward the wilderness. Though marching as one, the Israelites are probably wary as they enter into unknown territory, not sure of what other ethnic groups lie ahead. Like defenseless sheep, they are without weapons and are vulnerable. But God is with them and leads them along a safe path. They avoid the coastal land of the Philistines, a warrior nation who would intimidate the Israelites and drive them back to Egypt if encountered. God takes them south along the bottom of the Sinai Peninsula. This route will be a much longer trip than traveling along the Mediterranean Sea, but God will use this time to further establish His relationship with His people.

The Israelites move further and further from Egypt and into Succoth and Etham. Here, they pitch campsites to rest from the day's journey. Whether the Israelites are asleep or awake, God resides among them. He appears to them, clothed in a pillar of cloud during the day and of fire at night. His full glory would consume them otherwise. But, God desires to be with His people. A magnificent sight for the Israelites, the cloud and fire not only continue to emphasize the power of God but also provide comfort during a time of uncertainty.

Today's passage highlights the themes of holiness, worship, and God's abiding presence. Now free from bondage, the Israelites come into a relationship with the true God. We see that structures are necessary to maintain this freedom. Through the regulated holy days and animal sacrifices, the Israelites must remember how God was gracious to them and rescued them from slavery. The words of the Lord would be on their bodies to motivate a humble posture. Moses leads the Israelites in these ways of consecration to pursue holiness and worship. This consecration is made perfect in Jesus as the true substitutionary atonement for sin. Carrying our faults and standing in our place for judgment, He represented God's people. As the perfect human, His sacrifice was final. When we put our faith in Him, the work of Jesus consecrates us to the Lord by declaring us righteous, or faultless to God's law. Jesus then continues to consecrate us by making us more righteous, or like Him, day by day. This process is called sanctification. As we continue life's journey, the Spirit of Jesus reminds us of God's grace and love toward sinners. Like God's abiding presence in the cloud and fire, Jesus never leaves us to pursue holiness by ourselves. And through spiritual disciplines like Scripture memory and devotion, we engage in consecration by regularly meditating on His Word.

NOW FREE FROM BONDAGE, THE ISRAELITES COME INTO A RELATIONSHIP WITH THE TRUE GOD.

In what ways does Moses show godly leadership in this passage?

_____

_____

_____

_____

_____

_____

_____

_____

_____

How does consecration lead to worship?

_____

_____

_____

_____

_____

_____

What rhythms or habits should you incorporate to remember God's work
in your life?

_____

_____

_____

_____

_____

_____

_____

"BUT, AMONGST THE CROWD WHOSE FAITH IS ON QUICKSAND, MOSES STANDS FIRM."

WEEK 3 / DAY 3

Standing Firm

After a day's travel, the Lord leads Moses to the next campsite. He positions them in front of the Red Sea. Meanwhile in Egypt, Pharaoh's pride rears up again, and he goes back on his decision to let the Israelites go. Pharaoh assembles his skilled army and chariots and pursues them. He and his soldiers move quickly through the wilderness and spot them at their campsite by the sea. Seeing the Egyptians at a distance, the Israelites shudder with fear. When they see trouble approaching, the Israelites forget the almighty God is with them in the pillar of cloud and fire. They fear death, scorn Moses, and figure life would have been better if they had remained in slavery. Though out of Egypt, the people still have a natural inclination to long for the familiar, even if what is familiar is oppression. Their carnal desires keep them from trusting in God. But, amongst the crowd whose faith is on quicksand, Moses stands firm. Moses calls out to the people, "Don't be afraid. Stand firm and see the Lord's salvation that he will accomplish for you today…" (Exodus 14:13). He urges the people to trust in the Lord, for He will rescue them. God will complete His work of salvation here, and they will never see the Egyptians again. He says, "The Lord will fight for you, and you must be quiet" (Exodus 14:14). God's plan of salvation involves their faith and quiet trust in Him.

Upon the Lord's command, Moses tells the Israelites to pack up their campsite and head toward the Red Sea. The angel of God, a manifestation of His presence in the pillar of cloud and fire, creates a barrier and prevents the Egyptians from gaining ground. The Israelites reach the edge of the sea, likely staring in fear and uncertainty at the treacherous waves. Moses stretches his hand over the water, and the Lord sends a strong eastern wind to split the sea. The water parts, and a dry path emerges on the seafloor. In amazement, the Israelites go through the sea that is now raised like high walls on both sides.

Dawn approaches as the Israelites reach the other side of the sea. The pillar of cloud and fire sends the Egyptians into confusion. God strikes the chariots, causing them to swerve and collide. Some of the soldiers withdraw and cry out in defeat. But Pharaoh does not listen and sends more soldiers into the parted sea. After all of the Israelites have made it through, Moses stretches out his hand again, and the sea walls fall.

The water crashes down on the horsemen and chariots, drowning the entire army of Pharaoh. The Red Sea resumes its original depth, and the Israelites safely stand on the other side. In front of Pharaoh and spiritual evil, the Lord has showcased His power as the true God and secured salvation for His people. In witnessing this event, the Israelites put their faith in God and the authority given to Moses.

In today's passage, we see Moses leading the Israelites in their second exodus. Similar to the first exodus during Passover, the Lord helps them escape death. But this time Moses emphasizes the need for the Israelites to quietly trust in God. They must not give themselves over to fear but stand firm in the Lord's saving work. This epic part of Moses's story is the clearest picture of the victory that Jesus won for His people on the cross. Choosing Israel, enacting judgment on Pharaoh through the plagues, showing the Israelites mercy during the Passover, and freeing them from bondage so that they can worship God are all events pointing to the ultimate saving work of Jesus. Before the creation of the world, God chose a people, both Jews and Gentiles, to be in a relationship with Him. At the fall in the garden of Eden in Genesis 3, sin entered the world. Satan bound the heart of humanity toward selfishness, evil, and death. Hatred, lust, and injustice became innate, making us unable to please God or be in the presence of the Lord naturally. In Genesis 3:15, God set in motion a plan to liberate His people from sin. Jesus came as a substitutionary atonement to die for our sins. Because He was without sin, Jesus died as the perfect sacrifice. In His death, He received our due judgment, and we received mercy. In His resurrection, Jesus defeated Satan and broke sin's hold on us. Jesus Christ set us free, and now renewed, we can rest in God's presence and truly worship Him. Even when a threat comes and we wrestle with fear, we can always maintain quiet confidence in His salvation by remembering God's faithfulness in Jesus. We can call to mind His awesome power and glory. In still moments in God's presence, we can trust that no matter what terrifying circumstances we face, God will keep our spirits from harm.

GOD'S PLAN OF SALVATION INVOLVES THEIR FAITH AND QUIET TRUST IN HIM.

What is evidence of Moses's strengthened faith in this passage?

_____

_____

_____

_____

_____

_____

_____

_____

How does God involve Pharaoh's will in His plan of salvation?

_____

_____

_____

_____

_____

_____

_____

How can you remain firm in Jesus during times of adversity?

_____

_____

_____

_____

_____

_____

_____

"THOUGH NO LONGER PHYSICALLY CHAINED, THE HEARTS ARE STILL BOUND BY SIN."

WEEK 3 / DAY 4

The Redeemed Sing

Salvation results in doxology. Doxology is a structure for liturgy or public worship. This form is evident in the psalms, hymns, or other songs of praise. After seeing the Egyptians fall to the power of the Lord, Moses and the Israelites cannot contain their joy and overflow in exuberant praise on the sandy shores of the Red Sea. They lift their voices to the Lord as one. Their words proclaim God is their strength, song, and salvation. He is the covenant God of their ancestors. This is a victory poem, and God is the mighty warrior who has won the battle. Knowing His name, they proclaim Yahweh as the Holy God. He is unlike the gods of Egypt and the Canaanite god, Baal. The one true God has come to reclaim a place for His people and expel the rule of pagan idols. The Israelites' trust is bolstered. They know God will lead them to His holy dwelling place. They are His redeemed, a people freed from bondage and restored to His possession. He will cover them with His faithful love.

Moses and the Israelites remember the details of the event. Their song recites the water rising and falling by the breath of God and the sea crashing down on the Egyptian chariots. No other enemy will have a chance. They call out the Canaanite nations: Philistia, Edom, and Moab. All will hear of the Lord's great works and shudder when they see the Israelites travel throughout the region. They will fear the Lord and be still in their sight. God will lead the Israelites to His holy mountain. They will be planted in the place He prepared for them. Moses recalls the sanctity of Mount Horeb where he first met God in Exodus 3. He knows the mountain is associated with divine worship and will be the place from which God will rule. At the end of the song, the Israelites celebrate the Lord's reign and His eternal kingdom. God has kept His word to free the Israelites from slavery. He has kept His covenant promises to make Abraham's family into a great nation, bring them to the land of Canaan, and be their God forever. God has claimed a people, gifted His presence, and established a place for His glory.

Though the chorus song has concluded, the party does not cease. Aaron's sister, Miriam, leads the women in dancing, playing the tambourine, and singing. Scripture identifies her as a prophetess who must have awaited the Lord's salvation and preached of future deliverance through her younger brother, Moses. Surely Moses looks at the people who were once bitter and downcast and now sees their radiance, reflecting the honor and brilliance of the One who made them and keeps His covenants. But, how long would their disposition last? A shepherd knows his sheep. God knows the Israelites are celebrating now but will return to rebellion. Though no longer physically chained, their hearts are still bound by sin. But God will test the Israelites to refine them and prove their obedience.

Moses leads the Israelites through the Wilderness of Shur. For three days, they journey without water. The people are beginning to tire and weaken. They become restless and worried. At a place called Marah, they find a source of water but are unable to drink it. The water's bitter taste should remind them of the unpleasant life they left in Egypt and cause them to lean on the Lord for strength. But instead, they complain to Moses about their present troubles. They fail the first test in the wilderness. Moses prays to the Lord to provide refreshment for them, and He has Moses throw a tree in the water to make it drinkable. Again, God turns a bitter situation into a satisfying one. Though the Israelites did not trust Him, God still keeps His covenant. But He reveals that they must obey

to enjoy the covenant blessings. God is the initiator and sustainer of their covenant bond, but obedience is the expression of loyalty and love to God from the human side. If they disobey, the Israelites will suffer the same plagues sent to the Egyptians. After establishing the stipulations for the covenant, God takes them to Elim, a lush place full of spring water and date palm trees. He abundantly blesses them, giving them more than what they sought.

In today's passage, we see that Moses leads the people in a song to the Lord. The Lord's saving work was the reason for their praise. But moments later, under fatigue and dehydration, their singing quickly turns to grumbling. We too fall into the same habit. Our joys turn to bitterness, and we stop singing the Lord's praises when we focus too much on the things we lack rather than on the salvation we have received. But Jesus is our chief worship leader. He sings God's praises publicly (Hebrews 2:12). A song is always on His lips, and He leads us in worship (Matthew 26:30). Whether in times of strength or weakness, we should seek Jesus for a song to lift our gaze to Him and give us a spiritual perspective surpassing present circumstances.

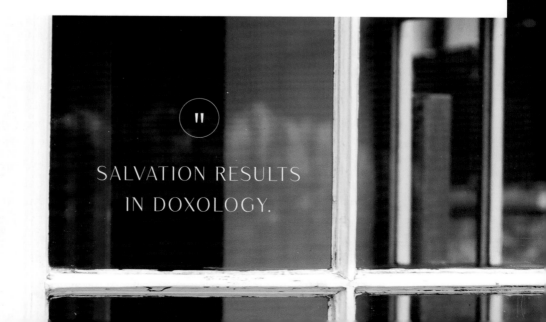

SALVATION RESULTS
IN DOXOLOGY.

What part of Moses's song stands out to you?

_____

_____

_____

_____

_____

_____

_____

_____

What does public worship show about our salvation in Jesus?

_____

_____

_____

_____

_____

_____

_____

_____

What song can you sing to the Lord today?

_____

_____

_____

_____

_____

_____

_____

_____

"JESUS DOES
NOT PERFORM
THESE MIRACLES
TO JUDGE,
BUT TO SAVE."

WEEK 3 / DAY 5

The Signs of Jesus

The ten plagues of Egypt showed the character and nature of the Lord. Each plague proved the God of the Israelites was the almighty God. Moses showed both Egyptians and Israelites signs and wonders from his shepherd's staff and by the stretch of his hand. But it was God's power that worked through him. In the Gospel of John, the disciple recounts seven signs and wonders witnessed in Jesus's ministry. These signs follow the same escalating structure as the signs in Exodus. However, Jesus does not perform these miracles to judge but to save. His redemptive work is restoring the people of God and establishing God's kingdom. Moses was the vehicle by which God delivered His people. Jesus is the vehicle and the source of divine deliverance. His signs show His glory as the Son of God who has come to save His people from their sins.

In chapter 2, John writes about Jesus's first sign—turning water into wine. Jesus, His mother, and disciples attend a wedding in Cana located in the region of Galilee. As the ceremony continues, they find there is no more wine for the guests. To relieve the hosts from embarrassment, Jesus's mother informs her son, likely hoping He will act to remedy the situation. Jesus concedes to His mother and tells the servants to fill six stone jars with water. These large containers are reserved for ceremonial washing according to the Jewish cleansing rituals. Jesus tells them to draw out the contents. They do and see that the water is now wine. The servants take some to the master of the ceremony who commends the groom for reserving the best wine for the end. This is the first time Jesus reveals His glory, and as a result, the faith of His disciples is strengthened. In this sign, Jesus shows that the time has come for the celebration. The stone jars and water are symbols of the uncleanness of sin and the human need for purification. Pure Himself, Jesus not only washes away our impurities but also gives us the sweet taste of His presence. He does so abundantly as illustrated in the overflowing amount of new wine in the jars. The water of the Nile turning to blood in Egypt symbolized death, but now Jesus turns water to wine to show pleasurable life in Him.

In chapter 6, John notes Jesus's fifth sign—walking on water. After feeding a crowd of over 5,000 with five loaves and two fish (the fourth sign), Jesus retreats to a mountain by Himself. His disciples go on ahead of Him to the Sea of Capernaum. They wait in a boat on the water. Darkness sets in, and a storm starts to brew. The wind turns the water. Though the waves are turbulent, the disciples row the boat through the storm. They look in the distance and see a figure walking on the water. It is Jesus, and He assures them to not be afraid. Jesus gets on the boat, and the storm settles. They can reach their destination safely. In this miracle, Jesus shows His power over nature. He can move on top of the sea. He will not be disturbed by the storm. Jewish travelers view the sea as dangerous and unknown, but Jesus shows He has authority over all things. The God who by His breath parted the Red Sea in Egypt is the same God who in human form stands on the Sea of Capernaum and does not succumb to the waves.

The seventh sign John records is the raising of Lazarus from the dead. The beginning of the account is sorrowful as Jesus mourns over the death of His friend. Jesus does not shed tears in hopelessness but grief over the effect of sin in the world. Jesus has the stone removed from the tomb. Martha, Lazarus's sister, tells Jesus there is an overwhelming stench from her brother being dead for four days. Jesus reminds Martha that He has come to show the glory of God; all she must do is believe. Jesus calls Lazarus out of the tomb with a loud voice. The dead man comes to life. Still wrapped in cloth, Lazarus walks out to the people. Through this sign, Jesus shows He is the one sent from heaven. He is the Son of God, equal to the Father in divinity. He restores the dead to life. In Exodus, the Egyptians suffered death in judgment for their sin and rebellion, but Jesus graciously gives His people life and power over death through His saving work and their belief.

The signs culminate in the ultimate sign—Jesus rising from the dead. In this finale, Jesus is resurrected from the grave. He accomplishes the task He was commissioned to perform by the Father, so the Father raises Him in glory and honor. At His resurrection, He pronounces victory over evil. In Christ, we witness the greatest sign and wonder: freedom from sin through the resurrection of Jesus Christ from the dead.

IN CHRIST, WE WITNESS THE GREATEST SIGN AND WONDER: FREEDOM FROM SIN THROUGH THE RESURRECTION OF JESUS CHRIST FROM THE DEAD.

What is the purpose of the seven signs written in John?

_____

_____

_____

_____

_____

_____

_____

_____

What do the signs reveal about the character and mission of Jesus?

_____

_____

_____

_____

_____

_____

How do the miracles of Jesus impact your faith?

_____

_____

_____

_____

_____

_____

_____

John's Seven Miracles of Jesus

TURNED WATER INTO WINE

John 2:1-11

HEALED AN OFFICIAL'S SON

John 4:46-54

MADE A DISABLED MAN WALK

John 5:1-9

FED THE 5,000

John 6:5-13

WALKED ON WATER

John 6:19-21

HEALED A MAN BORN BLIND

John 9:1-7

RAISED LAZARUS FROM THE DEAD

John 11:1-44

TODAY:

DRAW A PICTURE INSPIRED BY THE THEMES OF
DELIVERANCE AND FREEDOM.

I WILL BE WITH YOU
WHEN YOU PASS THROUGH
THE WATERS, AND WHEN
YOU PASS THROUGH THE
RIVERS, THEY WILL NOT
OVERWHELM YOU.

Isaiah 43:2a

Week 03 Reflection

Summarize the main points from this week's Scripture readings.

_____

_____

_____

_____

_____

_____

_____

_____

_____

_____

What did you observe from this week's passages about God and His character?

_____

_____

_____

_____

_____

_____

_____

_____

_____

_____

What do this week's passages reveal about the condition of mankind and yourself?

_____

_____

_____

_____

_____

_____

How do these passages point to the gospel?

_____

_____

_____

_____

_____

How should you respond to these Scriptures? What specific action steps can you take this week to apply them in your life?

_____

_____

_____

_____

_____

_____

_____

_____

Write a prayer in response to your study of God's Word. Adore God for who He is, confess sins that He revealed in your own life, ask Him to empower you to walk in obedience, and pray for anyone who comes to mind as you study.

_____

_____

_____

_____

_____

_____

_____

A Weary Mediator

"AS GOD'S REPRESENTATIVE TO THE PEOPLE, MOSES BRINGS DIRECTION AND DELIVERANCE."

WEEK 4 / DAY 1

Representing God to the People and the People to God

It has been nearly two months since the Israelites left Egypt, and now, food supplies are running low. To show their resentment, the entire Israelite community comes grumbling to Moses and Aaron (Exodus 16:2). The people are not simply bringing a complaint, but they are stirring up rebellion. They cry out that it would have been better to die full in Egypt than to die hungry in the wilderness. The Israelites assert a serious claim; they would rather have perished in the judgment of God than have been saved by His mercy. They show ingratitude for the Lord's redemption in their lives and claim they truly stand with Pharaoh.

God hears the grumbling of the Israelites and responds to address their needs. He tells Moses He will "rain bread from heaven" (Exodus 16:4). When bringing this word to the people, Moses criticizes them for being angry with his and Aaron's leadership. He claims they are upset with God. Moses clarifies his role as mediator. As God's representative to the people, Moses brings direction and deliverance, but he does not possess the sole authority to dictate what their journey to the Promised Land entails. Aaron tells them to bring their anger before God because He is present to hear their complaints. As Aaron is speaking, the glory of the Lord appears in a cloud. At this sight, it is probable that the Israelites do not utter a word. God speaks to Moses, telling him that the Israelites will be full and know Yahweh has satisfied them.

God supplies their food miraculously, giving them nourishment without any effort of their own. In the evening, quail come and rest on their campgrounds. The people can likely catch the birds easily. In the morning, dew turns into fine grain, called manna, for bread making. Though the quail comes only one time, the people are given manna every day, and they can gather just enough to feed the number of household members for each day. Some families take more than others, but each person receives the needed amount. When evening comes, there is no surplus or shortage. God's daily grace is sufficient for them. But there are some in the community who do not trust God to bring new manna each morning. They ration one day's supply and store the leftovers for later. As a result, the manna rots and attracts maggots. Moses is angry with them for their actions. These people do not realize that God is their ultimate provider, and they attempt to rely on themselves. However, their efforts come up short and bring death to their household.

When the sixth day comes, the Israelites gather a double portion of manna according to God's instruction. They are to bake and boil the food supply collected and keep it for tomorrow. The Lord has instituted "a holy Sabbath" (Exodus 16:23). On the Sabbath day, the Israelites will rest from their work and travels. God will also rest from providing manna that morning. Through this observance, God is setting the Israelites apart from the surrounding cultures. The Egyptians did not have a concept of a rest day during the week. As slaves in Egypt, the Israelites worked continuously, tiring their bodies and spirits from the nonstop labor. God is showing that He cares for physical and spiritual rejuvenation as well as productivity. Rest will also bring communion. Sustained by the sweet manna prepared the day before, the Israelites will have a dedicated time to be present with their households and together reflect on the goodness of God.

Unfortunately, some of the Israelites do not observe the Sabbath and go out to gather manna. But they do not find any. Work, not rest, is still a part of their rhythm. They think their efforts will sustain them, and they ignore the time of rest that would point them to the true Sustainer. The Lord comes to Moses and rebukes the Israelites by asking, "How long will you refuse to keep my commands and instructions?" (Exodus 16:28). As the covenant mediator, Moses also represents the people of Israel to God. He bears the brunt of God's chastisement on the Israelites' behalf. Moses takes this message back to the Israelites, emphasizing the importance of the Sabbath. They will commemorate this time in the wilderness by collecting a portion of the manna and placing it before the Lord. They will remember that God supplied their need by His daily provision.

In today's reading, we begin to see Moses operate as the covenant mediator. Because God is holy, His covenant is maintained through intercession which occurs when a chosen representative steps in, advocates, and petitions for the blessing of God's people. Moses goes before both the Lord and the Israelites to relay God's command and bring the sins of the people to God. Jesus is the true covenant mediator, who, as the sacrificial Lamb, never stops interceding on our behalf in the Father's presence. Jesus is also the Bread of Life (John 6:35). He is the manna sent from heaven whose broken body sustains us and gives us eternal life.

AS THE COVENANT MEDIATOR, MOSES ALSO REPRESENTS THE PEOPLE OF ISRAEL TO GOD.

How is Moses handling his role as a mediator so far?

_____

_____

_____

_____

_____

_____

_____

_____

When do you attempt to sustain yourself by your own effort?

_____

_____

_____

_____

_____

_____

_____

_____

In what ways has God provided in your life?

_____

_____

_____

_____

_____

_____

_____

_____

"THE ROCK
WAS BROKEN,
JUST AS JESUS'S
BODY WAS
BROKEN FOR
OUR SINS."

WEEK 4 / DAY 2

On the Rock

Though the Israelites failed the test in the Wilderness of Sin, God still advances them toward Canaan. At the Lord's command, Moses leads them on to the next place, Rephidim. Here, the Israelites find themselves in a similar situation as before. They are in a desert place with no water. Although knowing God provided spring water for them in Elim, the Israelites still complain. They approach Moses with a demand. Moses shrinks as the Israelites surround him. "Give us water to drink," they order. Moses asks the people why they are complaining. Has not the Lord already shown His glory? Why do you not seek and trust Him? In his questioning, Moses asserts that the Israelites are testing the Lord. They are putting God on trial to see whether or not He will come to their aid. The Israelites seem to assume superiority over God and believe He should respond to their call. The people's thirst for water reveals their thirst to be their god. The crowd grows in anger and accuses Moses of trying to kill them by dehydration. Moses seems to believe that they want to stone him, so He runs to God in fear of his life.

The Lord answers Moses with a solution to their need. He sees that the Israelites are not trusting His word and authority, but He remains patient. God uses each failed test to reveal the sinfulness of the human heart and reveal His merciful character. Even though He does not owe anything to the Israelites, He seeks their good because of His commitment to His word. As the Lord commands, Moses chooses some of the elders and passes in front of the people. Scholars believe this walking before the community shows that Moses and the elders are representing the people. They stand in place of the twelve tribes of Israel before the rock at Horeb. Moses not only stands among them but also holds up his staff that was used to part the Red Sea. The staff is a symbol of God's power and judgment. He stretches it toward the rock. God descends in front of Moses onto the rock. Scripture does not give details on the Lord's appearance, but it is clear that the invisible God is present. Moses brings down his staff, striking the rock on which God stands. Streams of water begin to flow from the broken crevices.

Sometime after their thirst is satisfied, the Israelites encounter an attack at Rephidim. The Amalekites, a nation living near the region of Canaan, become another enemy for the Israelites. Moses calls for his assistant, Joshua, to select men from the community and fight against the Amalekites. After a day of warring, Moses takes Aaron and their brother-in-law, Hur, and goes up to the hill to overlook the armies. Moses knows the power of God and trusts in Him for help. Remembering the defeat of the Egyptians, Moses lifts his staff in faith that God will support them. The raised staff is a sign of a victory already won. God sees Moses's faith and gives them an advantage. As Moses keeps his hand raised, the Israelites prevail and push the Amalekites back. As time goes on, Moses begins to grow tired. His hands start to fall, lowering the staff from the sky. Aaron and Hur see that this causes the Amalekites to gain ground. They quickly grab a rock for Moses to rest on, and they keep his arms lifted. By sundown, God gives Joshua victory, and the Amalekites are defeated. Instead of a song, this time, Moses builds an altar to worship the Lord. He names it "The Lord Is My Banner." The Israelites may not have a flag to show their strength like the other nations do, but God is their banner because He is the source of strength, and with Him, they will not fail.

Today's reading uses rock imagery to illustrate the mediator role. Moses is the representative of the people. He embodies their sinfulness when he passes in front of them at Horeb. Moses also represents God. His extended staff toward the rock embodies divine wrath and judgment. Fully man, Jesus is our true representative and takes on our sins. Fully God, He allowed our sin to wound Him on the cross. He received the wrath and judgment we deserved from the Father. The rock was broken, just as Jesus's body was broken for our sins. But through His death, He gives us water for eternal life.

GOD IS THEIR BANNER BECAUSE
HE IS THE SOURCE OF STRENGTH,
AND WITH HIM, THEY WILL NOT FAIL.

Why was it wrong for the Israelites to test God?

_____
_____
_____
_____
_____
_____
_____
_____
_____

Read Isaiah 53:5. For what sins was Jesus's body broken?

_____
_____
_____
_____
_____
_____
_____

Recount a time when the Lord was your banner (a sign of strength) when you faced a difficult situation.

_____
_____
_____
_____
_____
_____
_____
_____

"THROUGH HIS JUDICIAL DECISIONS, MOSES ALSO TEACHES GOD'S LAW AND STANDARD FOR JUST LIVING."

WEEK 4 / DAY 3

Judging and Teaching God's Law

After the Israelites defeat the Amalekites in battle, Moses reunites with his father-in-law, Jethro. He has come to hear all of what Yahweh has done for His people. Moses recounts for him their journey and emphasizes how the Lord has kept them every step of the way. In response, Jethro's faith is strengthened. The priest of Midian proclaims, "Now I know that the Lord is greater than all gods" (Exodus 18:11). Though already acquainted with Yahweh, Jethro is still inspired by Moses's testimony. In worship, Jethro brings a sacrifice before the Lord, and they host a celebratory meal in God's presence. This is a sweet family reunion — eating good food and being in good company while reflecting on the goodness of God.

The next day, Jethro sees Moses in his leadership role. Moses now acts as a judge, settling conflicts among the Israelites. The people swarm him with their problems from morning to evening. Through his judicial decisions, Moses also teaches God's law and standard for just living. As covenant people, the Israelites must conduct themselves in ways that show their love for God and each other. Concerned about his well-being, Jethro questions why Moses is alone in this task. Jethro urges him to select discerning men with integrity to judge minor cases on his behalf. Jethro is wise and knows that to be a good leader, Moses must accept his weaknesses. Ministry is a team effort. Delegating tasks is essential for the health of a leader and gives others opportunities to serve.

Refreshed from time spent with his family, Moses then leads the people to the Sinai Wilderness. The Spirit of God descends upon the mountain there and calls to Moses. Moses follows the voice of God and enters His presence. The Lord expresses His affection for the Israelites. God says, "I carried you on eagles' wings" (Exodus 19:4). This metaphor paints a picture of the Israelites soaring on the most majestic bird in the sky. He then reveals His desire to bless them if they remain in a relationship with Him. The Lord states, "you will be my own possession out of all the peoples, although the whole earth is mine, and you will be my kingdom of priests and my holy nation" (Exodus

19:5-6). God redeemed the Israelites to restore the covenant bond with His creation. This bond was fractured during the fall of Adam and Eve in Genesis 3. God chose to reestablish this bond and selected the Israelites to be the people to whom He would commit Himself. But to enjoy the blessings of this relationship, the Israelites will need to be faithful. The nation of Israel will gain the role of priest-king to steward the Lord's dwelling place and point the rest of the world to the one true God. This title once belonged to Adam as he was created to protect God's dwelling place in Eden and defend the word of the Lord. But, because of his desire to be his own master and his distrust in God, he failed to perform as priest-king and lost the life he enjoyed in God's presence. The Israelites must not follow the ways of their first parents. They must pursue obedience and holiness in love and gratitude for the salvation they received.

Moses comes down from the mountain to consecrate the Israelites. The people wash their clothes to reflect God's purity, and they prepare their hearts for the Lord's descension. On their third day in Sinai, the sky grows dark, and thunder and lightning appear. At the sound of a trumpet from heaven, a thick cloud emerges and covers the mountain. Moses leads the people from the camp to the bottom of the mountain so that they can meet their God. The

mountain shakes, and fire and smoke roar from its top. The Israelites tremble in awe of their Lord. After telling the Israelites not to break through the barrier, Moses enters the thick cloud and goes up to receive the Lord's word. Moses will meet with the just God who will graciously give the people His written law so that they will know how to live in a covenant relationship with Him.

In today's passages, we see Moses act as judge, and we learn that for the Israelites to enjoy the blessings of their salvation, they must pursue holiness and righteousness. Righteousness is the measure of one's ability to live up to God's law. Moses communicates this law to the people. The Israelites must live set apart from pagan nations by loving and obeying Yahweh. But Jesus, the Son of God, is both the true judge and the one who has obeyed God's law perfectly. When we believe in His life, death, and resurrection, we inherit His perfect record and receive the blessings of a restored covenant relationship with God. We still pursue righteousness out of hearts that have been transformed in Christ. We can ask the Holy Spirit to help us keep our eyes on the perfection of Jesus when we fall short of God's standard and trust He will one day perfect us.

TO ENJOY THE BLESSINGS OF THIS RELATIONSHIP, THE ISRAELITES WILL NEED TO BE FAITHFUL.

Moses testifies of the Lord's work to free the Israelites, and Jethro is blessed by his sharing. Take some time to write out your testimony of how God has worked in your life. Is there someone you can share your testimony with this week?

_____

_____

_____

_____

_____

_____

_____

Are there areas in your life where you can involve the help of others to assist you in your service to God?

_____

_____

_____

_____

_____

_____

Read Psalm 119:1-16. Write out a prayer, asking God to help you find delight in His law.

_____

_____

_____

_____

_____

_____

_____

"YOUR PERFECTION
IS NOT REQUIRED,
BUT YOUR
FAITH IN JESUS'S
PERFECTION IS."

WEEK 4 / DAY 4

Interceding for Mercy

After entering the thick cloud on Mount Sinai, Moses receives God's laws, part of which is the Ten Commandments. These laws, etched in stone, are universal commands for loving God and people. But before giving His law, God reminds them that He is the God who brought them out of slavery and into freedom and rest. The law is given after God initiated and established their relationship with Him. God's grace, not their obedience to the law, secures their salvation. However, for the Israelites to enjoy their new life fully, they must adhere to God's law that brings wisdom, peace, and protection. In chapter 24, the Israelites agree to obey the word of the Lord who rescued them.

Moses stays on Mount Sinai for forty days. Meanwhile, the Israelites are becoming impatient. In Moses's absence, the people decide to take matters into their own hands. They tell Aaron to make an idol god to be their leader instead, and he concedes. He takes their gold jewelry and fashions a golden calf. When the Israelites see this image, they distort covenant truth and give the calf idol the honor of God's salvation. They have broken the first commandment, "Do not have other gods besides me" (Exodus 20:3). Aaron sees his error and builds an altar. He declares that the next day, they will have a festival for Yahweh. But the people rise early with desires to party in the name of their calf idol. God sees their presumption and disgraceful acts. He orders Moses to leave Him alone so He can destroy them for their rebellion. God is just and is righteously angry toward ungrateful creatures who disobey His law. But, in His dialogue with Moses, God reveals His mercy. God uses judgment to rouse Moses to seek forgiveness. In response to God's wrath, Moses asks the Lord to remember His covenant commitment. He urges God to remember Israel, the nation He carried on eagles' wings out of Egypt (Exodus 19:4). As a result of Moses's intercession, God relents, meaning He displays His mercy, not that He changes His mind. God knew the Israelites would commit this idolatry, and it was His gracious plan to show both His just and merciful character through Moses's intercession.

Moses then descends Mount Sinai with the Ten Commandments on two stone tablets. He becomes enraged when he hears the sound of partying in the Israelite camp. He smashes the stone tablets at the base of the mountain, for the Israelites have broken the law and have not loved the true God who has loved them. He then takes the calf, burns it, and turns it into powder. He puts the powder in water and makes the people drink it. The Israelites are made to taste the bitter water, likely to realize how displeasing their idolatry is to God. Moses confronts Aaron for his poor leadership, but he avoids responsibility and claims that Moses should not be surprised since the people are inclined to rebel. Certainly, in this moment, it is probable that Moses feels alone in his anger toward sin. Will there be anyone else who stands with God? Moses looks around at the revelry and stands up at the camp's entrance to bring it all to an end. Moses calls out to the crowd, "Whoever is for the Lord, come to me" (Exodus 32:26). The Levites, including Aaron, come to Moses's side. They repent of their sin, and upon Moses's command, they kill the men who refuse to follow God.

Though God showed His mercy and the people repented, the Israelites still have a debt that needs to be repaid. Moses returns to the mountain to see if he can atone, or make a payment, for their sins. Moses asks God for forgiveness and offers to lay down his life as a substitutionary atonement. He asks the Lord to take his life instead of punishing the people. But there are limits to Moses's role as intercessor and repre-sentative. Instead, God says each person will be accountable for his or her sins and sends a plague as judgment. Moses himself cannot serve as a substitutionary atonement for the people because he too is sinful and imperfect. God's people need a sacrificial savior who is completely blameless and righteous. Surely, Moses longs for this true representative as he continues to lead the Israelites to the Promised Land.

In today's passage, we see the persistence of sin in the human heart and our need for a savior to erase our debt. Moses was not able to atone for the Israelites. But perfect atonement is accomplished by Jesus Christ. His sacrifice absolves our past, present, and future sins. Like the Israelites tasting the bitterness of their idolatry, we should come face to face with the gravity of our rebellion and pride. Today, by God's grace, there is an opportunity for repentance and to stand on the Lord's side. Though you may feel shame for your actions, God still wants to bless you with the fullness of life in relationship with Him. Your perfection is not required, but your faith in Jesus's perfection is. No sin is too great for the blood of Jesus. Jesus has interceded and taken the punishment we deserved. Through Jesus's intercession, in His faithfulness and love, the Father extends us mercy.

GOD'S PEOPLE NEED A SACRIFICIAL SAVIOR WHO IS COMPLETELY BLAMELESS AND RIGHTEOUS.

DO NOT HAVE OTHER
GODS BESIDES ME.

DO NOT MAKE, WORSHIP,
OR SERVE IDOLS.

DO NOT MISUSE THE NAME
OF THE LORD YOUR GOD.

REMEMBER THE SABBATH
DAY TO KEEP IT HOLY.

HONOR YOUR FATHER
AND YOUR MOTHER.

DO NOT MURDER.

DO NOT COMMIT
ADULTERY.

DO NOT STEAL.

DO NOT GIVE FALSE
TESTIMONY AGAINST
YOUR NEIGHBOR.

DO NOT COVET ANYTHING
THAT BELONGS TO
YOUR NEIGHBOR.

In what ways are the Israelites replaying the fall of Adam and Eve in Genesis 3?

_____

_____

_____

_____

_____

How does Moses use his passion and righteous anger constructively in this passage?

_____

_____

_____

_____

Confess ways you have followed your own heart this week. How does the gospel
free you from guilt and shame?

_____

_____

_____

_____

_____

"JESUS PROVES TO BE THE ONLY ONE FAITHFUL TO GOD THE FATHER AND WORTHY OF THE COVENANT BLESSINGS."

WEEK 4 / DAY 5

READ MATTHEW 5, JOHN 17:20-26

Fulfilling the Law

This week, we observed how Moses performed his role as intercessor. But a sinner himself, Moses was not able to perfectly atone for the Israelites' idol worship of the golden calf. Moses's limited role pointed to the need for a true intercessor who would fully reveal the character of God, obey the law perfectly, and sacrifice himself to pay for the debts of God's people. In today's passages, the gospel writers prove that Jesus is this true intercessor. In His sermon on the mountain, Jesus reveals God's intent behind the law given through Moses on Mount Sinai. Then, Jesus intimately prays for God's people, seeking to bring them into union with Him and with the Father.

In Matthew 5, Jesus ascends a mountain and sits among His disciples. In this way, He mirrors Moses who ascended Mount Sinai to receive God's law. But here, Jesus is the one teaching a new law. He lays out certain ethics that define the people of God. He identifies the inner dispositions of purity, humility, longsuffering, righteousness, mercy, and peace. Jesus calls the lowly and meek "blessed." The repetition of this word points back to covenant language. Faith exercised in obedience to God's commands is the requirement for covenant people. The results are blessings of life and rest in His presence and His holy land. Initially, God's people would show their faithfulness by following the Ten Commandments and the other ceremonial and civil laws given at Mount Sinai. These were not oppressive commands, but they were standards graciously given so that the Israelites could rightly love God and others. Unfortunately, throughout the generations leading to the coming of Jesus, God's people continue to fall short of God's law, proving that the real problem is sin in the human heart. Even those who appear to obey the law, like the religious leaders of Jesus's time, do so out of selfish motives and not out of humility or reverence for God.

In his sermon on the mountain, Jesus teaches the true intent for the law. He shows that the character of one's heart is more important than outward signs. Jesus teaches that those who do not sin in their hearts will receive mercy, rest, comfort, a new identity, righteousness, and life in the kingdom of God. He teaches a radical love in which the people of God love their enemies and become servants, putting others' needs before their own. He also speaks of the kingdom of heaven rather than the

Promised Land that God had spoken of in His covenant with the Israelites. In doing so, Jesus reveals that the blessing of covenant is more than a national government for the Jewish people. Instead, the Holy Land that Moses and the Israelites were traveling to in Exodus is a picture of God's spiritual dwelling place where He reigns as King. Jesus declares that the kingdom of heaven would be rewarded to those who possess the inner dispositions and the servant heart He identified. Jesus brings the covenant and law of the Old Testament into light. His new law reveals what is ultimately required for the covenant blessing—a sinless heart. Additionally, Jesus displays the full glory of the covenant promises—eternal life in God's presence.

Jesus clarifies to His disciples that He has not come to abolish the law given through Moses but to fulfill it (Matthew 5:17). Fulfilling the law means that Jesus accomplishes all of what the old covenant requires. In His obedience, He follows the Ten Commandments and fulfills the civil and ceremonial laws. He lives blamelessly and does not commit any sin in His heart. He possesses meekness, humility, love, peace, purity, and righteousness. Through His sacrifice, He completes Old Testament prophecies which predict there would be One sent from heaven, the Son of God, who would die to pay for the sins of God's people. During His life and service, Jesus proves to be the only one faithful to God the Father and worthy of the covenant blessings.

But what does Jesus revealing and fulfilling the law now mean for future believers like us? We continue to sin inwardly, failing to live up to the kingdom ethics in Matthew 5, and it may be difficult to see how God's covenant applies to us. In John 17, Jesus, the true intercessor, invites us into a covenant relationship by praying for our union with Him. In this union, the great exchange occurs. As our perfect representative, fully God and fully human, Jesus takes our punishment for sin, and He gives us His perfect record. In this prayer to God the Father, Jesus reveals the covenant of redemption, the plan to redeem God's people, which the triune God established in the eternity past. In verses 20-26, Jesus prays that through faith in Him, we as future believers would receive the covenant blessings and glory He was rewarded for His faithfulness. Also, Jesus prays that the love of God and His own Spirit dwells in our hearts so that we would overcome sin and become people with kingdom of heaven ethics.

JESUS, THE TRUE INTERCESSOR, INVITES US INTO A COVENANT RELATIONSHIP BY PRAYING FOR OUR UNION WITH HIM.

Read Hebrews 9:15. What does it mean that "Jesus is the mediator of a new covenant"?

What kingdom of heaven ethic in Matthew 5 challenges you?

How do you react to know that the true Intercessor prayed for you in John 17:20-26?

The Beatitudes

Matthew 5:3-10

BLESSED ARE THE POOR IN SPIRIT,
for the kingdom of heaven is theirs.

BLESSED ARE THOSE WHO MOURN,
for they will be comforted.

BLESSED ARE THE HUMBLE,
for they will inherit the earth.

BLESSED ARE THOSE WHO HUNGER AND
THIRST FOR RIGHTEOUSNESS,
for they will be filled.

BLESSED ARE THE MERCIFUL,
for they will be shown mercy.

BLESSED ARE THE PURE IN HEART,
for they will see God.

BLESSED ARE THE PEACEMAKERS,
for they will be called sons of God.

BLESSED ARE THOSE WHO ARE PERSECUTED
BECAUSE OF RIGHTEOUSNESS,
for the kingdom of heaven is theirs.

DEATH WAS APPROACHING, A THIEF IN THE NIGHT
THE SON OF GOD THE SOLDIERS SOUGHT TO FIND
SATAN SLITHERED AND SAW THE HEEL TO BITE
BUT, IN THIS DARKNESS, YOU WERE ON HIS MIND

KNEELING, JESUS WENT TO THE THRONE OF GRACE
TO INTERCEDE WHERE YOU HAVE FALLEN SHORT
HE PRAYED FOR YOU TO KNOW GOD FACE TO FACE
THROUGH HIS BLOOD PRESENTED IN HEAVEN'S COURT

HE PRAYED FOR HIS SPIRIT IN YOU TO DWELL
UNION WITH JESUS, SALVATION FROM SIN
GOD'S GREAT LOVE TOWARDS YOU EVIL CANNOT QUELL
BETWEEN US AND GOD HE IS THE LINCHPIN

Kyra Daniels

SCRIPTURE MEMORY

04

FOR I AM PERSUADED THAT NEITHER DEATH NOR LIFE, NOR ANGELS NOR RULERS, NOR THINGS PRESENT NOR THINGS TO COME, NOR POWERS, NOR HEIGHT NOR DEPTH, NOR ANY OTHER CREATED THING WILL BE ABLE TO SEPARATE US FROM THE LOVE OF GOD THAT IS IN CHRIST JESUS OUR LORD.

Romans 8:38-39

Week 04 Reflection

Summarize the main points from this week's Scripture readings.

_____
_____
_____
_____
_____
_____
_____
_____
_____
_____
_____
_____

What did you observe from this week's passages about God and His character?

_____
_____
_____
_____
_____
_____
_____
_____
_____
_____
_____
_____

What do this week's passages reveal about the condition of mankind and yourself?

_____
_____
_____
_____
_____
_____

How do these passages point to the gospel?

_____

_____

_____

_____

_____

How should you respond to these Scriptures? What specific action steps can you take this week to apply them in your life?

Write a prayer in response to your study of God's Word. Adore God for who He is, confess sins that He revealed in your own life, ask Him to empower you to walk in obedience, and pray for anyone who comes to mind as you study.

Blessing the Tabernacle

WEEK FIVE

"IN JESUS, WE HAVE CONFIDENCE THAT GOD'S DISPOSITION TOWARD US IS GOOD, EVEN WHEN WE FALL SHORT."

WEEK 5 / DAY 1

The Friend of God

After the plague passes, the Israelites emerge out of the rubble and ruin. Scripture is not specific about the impact of the plague on the camp or if there was any life lost as a result, but it is clear that what remains is a broken relationship with God. Perhaps knowing that the plague God sent was a just punishment for their idol worship of the golden calf, it does not seem that the people voice claims of unfair treatment. The Israelites appear to realize the goodness and righteousness of God's justice and feel the weight of their sin. The Lord comes to Moses and tells him to continue the journey to the land of Canaan with the people Moses brought out of Egypt. God does not claim the Israelites as His people but hands them over to Moses. Like a marriage trust that has been betrayed by adultery, the covenant relationship has been violated. But God is still faithful to His promises and will still give the Israelites the Promised Land. Instead of journeying with the Israelites through the wilderness, however, He will send an angel ahead to prepare the land for their settlement. Since the Israelites are corrupted by their moral impurity, the Holy God cannot dwell in their midst lest the people be destroyed by His glory. God is not throwing a tantrum, but He is protecting them and showing that the result of sin is separation from God. When the people hear of this news, they mourn and do not put on jewelry, the object that likely reminds them of their sin. The people are remorseful instead of joyful. Though they will still receive the bountiful land, Canaan, they know what they need and desire most of all is God.

Separation from God leads Moses to intercede. On Mount Sinai, Moses had received God's instructions on building the tabernacle, an ornate and portable tent structure in which God would dwell on the route to Canaan. The thought of God no longer dwelling in the center of the camp troubles Moses. He knows he is unable to lead the people through the wilderness by himself. He goes to God to speak about his concerns. At a distance from the people, Moses pitches a makeshift tent outside the campsite, called the Tent of Meeting. With his assistant, Joshua, at his side, Moses enters the structure, and God clothed in a pillar of cloud descends at the tent's entrance. The people, far away from this encounter, are grateful for the Lord's distant appearance and are moved to worship. Inside the tent, God speaks with Moses face to face which is an expression for His intimate presence. They speak like one friend to another. Moses is vulnerable and pours out his heart to the loving God. Moses expresses that the Israelites are God's people. Moses knows the goal of the covenant is intimacy with God, not a territorial occupation. Moses also emphasizes his desire to know God the way God knows him. Though Moses has a special relationship with God, he is still limited in his understanding. By His affection toward Moses, the faithful mediator, God says He will give Moses rest. Scholars note that use of the singular pronoun "you" in these verses suggests that God is promising to Moses alone. God will give Moses peace to ease his worries about leading. Moses responds to include the Israelites as recipients of God's favor. To radiate God's glory to the nations, Moses pleads for God to go with them. Revealing His faithfulness, God concedes to Moses's intercession. Because of God's favor and intimate relationship with Moses, God will also show the Israelites favor and restore relational harmony.

In today's passage, we see two important narrative elements: Moses's inability to lead the people alone and the intimacy between God and Moses. Moses knows He needs divine assistance on the route to Canaan. He pleads for the Lord's loving presence and protection to complete his mission. But, to save His people from sin and bring them to His kingdom, God Himself in the person of Jesus Christ completes this mission. In Jesus, God clothed Himself in flesh and dwelt among His people. Now, the Spirit of Jesus continues to dwell in our hearts, continuing God's redemptive mission until Jesus's return. Secondly, the intimacy between God and Moses shows that relational reconciliation with God happens through the beloved mediator who asks for God's mercy. Through the intimate relationship between the Father and Jesus, we see that God not only bestows favor but also advocates for it. In Jesus, we have confidence that God's disposition toward us is good, even when we fall short. God ultimately seeks our wellbeing and restoration from sin. Through the intercession and saving work of Jesus, we know that God is our advocate and looks favorably upon us. We are friends of God (John 15:15), and we can trust that in the unfailing bond between the Father and Son, we can also have peace and intimacy with God.

THROUGH THE INTERCESSION AND SAVING WORK OF JESUS, WE KNOW THAT GOD IS OUR ADVOCATE AND LOOKS FAVORABLY UPON US.

When was a time you felt separated from God due to sin?

How could seeing God as a friend affect your prayer life?

How does Moses's pursuit to witness God's glory move your pursuit to know God?

"GOD'S JEALOUSY
IS FUELED BY
HIS PASSIONATE
LOVE TOWARD
HIS CREATION."

WEEK 5 / DAY 2

Radiating God's Glory

In Chapter 33, Moses asks for God to reveal His glory so he can more deeply know the Lord's nature. God agrees to let His goodness pass in front of Moses. God will declare His eternal name and attributes. The Lord displays His sovereignty in selectively revealing His glory to the chosen mediator. But, because humans are not able to see the fullness of God's glory, God will hide Moses in the crevice of a rock when He appears. He will protect Moses from the power of His holiness. Then, when it is safe, God will remove His hand to give a partial view. Moses will see the Lord's back. The use of "back" is an intentional word choice to express that God's glory was withheld.

Before showing this theophany which is a visible manifestation of His presence, the Lord reestablishes the covenant. God tells Moses to cut two stone tablets for the Ten Commandments to replace the first ones he shattered. At first, God had provided the stone tablets Himself (Exodus 31:18). But, representing the people, Moses will provide the stones this time, perhaps to show that the Israelites are serious about their relationship with the Lord. Like in rebuilding a marriage union, the adulterous spouse must show a renewed commitment and loyalty to the other. God then tells Moses to bring these tablets to Mount Sinai the next morning, and no individual or animal can come near the mountain. The holiness of God cannot be defiled by any sinner. In this covenant renewal, the people must show reverence for the God who has come near.

Moses gets up early the next day and ascends Mount Sinai with the two stone tablets in hand. The Lord comes down in a pillar of cloud, and His glory fills the mountaintop. With Moses hiding behind the rock and protected by the hand of God, the Lord passes in front of Moses. His goodness radiates from behind the cloud. God answers Moses's prayer to know who He is. The Lord declares, "The Lord—the Lord is a compassionate and gracious God, slow to anger and abounding in faithful love and truth, maintaining faithful love to a thousand generations, forgiving iniquity, rebellion, and sin. But He will not leave the guilty unpunished, bringing the fathers' iniquity on the children and grandchildren to the third and fourth generation" (Exodus 34:6-7). In response to this declaration of the Lord's love, righteousness, and justice, Moses falls to the ground in worship. He calls on God to act on the truth of who He is and accept the Israelites back as His possession.

God draws Moses's attention to the covenant that He is reinstating. He promises to do wondrous miracles for the Israelites and to drive their enemies out of Canaan. God calls the Israelites to live holy lives and not to follow in the ways of the pagan nations. Their false worship will be a temptation for the Israelites. God addresses their weakness and emphasizes their adherence to the first two commandments: do not have other gods besides me, and do not make an idol for yourself. God reveals that He is a jealous God. This jealousy is not like human jealousy which is based on envy and selfishness. Instead, God's jealousy is fueled by His passionate love toward His creation. His zeal seeks human good and protection. God's jealousy is selfless as He desires to keep from harm what is most valuable to Him. Therefore, the covenant obligations are not random conditions, but they intentionally address the sin issues in the hearts of the people, and the restrictions point the Israelites back to right worship of the true God.

As a result of Moses speaking to the Lord for forty days and nights, his face shines and radiates the glory of God. Moses descends with the two stone tablets on which God wrote the Ten Commandments. This time, Instead of coming upon a party, Moses comes to the Israelite camp who is in fear and awe of Moses's appearance. No one comes near his light, but Moses tells them to draw closer so he can relay God's word. They all listen and respect Moses's authority. After speaking with them, Moses covers his face with a veil until he goes to speak with the Lord again.

In today's passage, we see that God uses the intercession of Moses to reveal the depths of His character. God foreknew the Israelites would transgress the covenant, but He allowed them to do so because their idolatry would ultimately lead to the declaration of God's goodness. There are idols in our hearts as well—wealth, social status, career success, or pleasures, among many others. But, when exposed, they show our moral weaknesses and our need to depend on Jesus's perfect worship. We come to Jesus who displays the full glory of God, surpassing the fading radiance Moses was given. In Christ, by the Holy Spirit, we with unveiled faces look upon the fullness of God's glory and are given Jesus's radiant image (2 Corinthians 3:18).

IN CHRIST, BY THE HOLY SPIRIT, WE WITH UNVEILED FACES LOOK UPON THE FULLNESS OF GOD'S GLORY AND ARE GIVEN JESUS'S RADIANT IMAGE.

How do you react to this glorious revelation of God's character in Exodus 34:6-7?

_____

_____

_____

_____

_____

_____

_____

_____

Identify idols of your heart that are affecting your walk with the Lord.

_____

_____

_____

_____

_____

_____

_____

Read Hebrews 1:3 and 2 Corinthians 3:7-18. How does the new covenant mediated by Jesus radiate the full glory of God?

_____

_____

_____

_____

_____

_____

_____

_____

"THE ISRAELITES REALIZE THEY ARE UNDESERVING SINNERS AND ARE SO GRATEFUL FOR GOD'S COVENANT FAITHFULNESS."

WEEK 5 / DAY 3

Restoring the Covenant Bond

After receiving the Ten Commandments on new stone tablets, Moses descends Mount Sinai and returns to the camp to restore the covenant relationship between God and the people. He relays the standard to which the Israelites must adhere. They must resist the temptation of idolatry and trust in God's lovingkindness to enjoy the blessing of His presence. Through Moses, Yahweh reemphasizes the Sabbath command which is to dedicate the seventh day of the week as a day of rest before the Lord. After six days of labor, the Israelites are to enjoy a repose for their physical and spiritual wellbeing. The Sabbath is a time for them to savor the sweet presence of God, fellowship with others, and rest in their identity as God's possession. Reinstating the Sabbath command shows that God still desires communion, even after the betrayal of the golden calf. Through Moses's intercession as a mediator, God heals what was broken and reveals His commitment to dwell among His people. After hearing this news from Moses, what a relief this must be for the Israelites. They can continue the journey to the Promised Land with the glory of the true God in their midst.

Moses moves forward with the Lord's instructions to build the tabernacle, a portable and large tent structure where the glory of the Lord would abide. Instead of coming and going on mountaintops, the Lord would rest in the center of the Israelite camp permanently. And the tabernacle would radiate the light of God to surrounding nations, establishing God's kingdom on earth and calling others to Him. Moses invites the Israelites to contribute to the construction of the tabernacle. He takes up an offering from among the people. Those whose hearts are willing (Exodus 35:5) bring Moses gold, silver, bronze, gemstones, yarn, fine linen, acacia wood, spices, oil, and fragrance. Some scholars suggest that some of these luxurious materials were a part of the items given by Egyptians as the Israelites were fleeing (Exodus 12:35-36). What was used for man's opulence in Egypt is now used for God's glory in His dwelling place. Also, gold that had been fashioned together for the calf statue is no longer associated with idol worship. Instead, gold has been reclaimed to show the beauty of God's divine presence.

The people bring this offering out of gratitude for God's forgiveness and restoration. God's grace moves their hearts to give generously. God softens their hearts so that they understand the severity of their sin and the magnitude of the Lord's kindness. The Israelites must realize they are undeserving sinners and are so grateful for God's covenant faithfulness. Though no gift will be enough to repay the Lord, they freely give back to Him an offering of thankfulness. Their gratitude moves them not only to bring the items but also to prepare them. Both men and women ready raw materials for use. Skilled women spin fibers and animal hair to make yarn and linen. Every morning, the people bring and prepare an overwhelming number of items for the tabernacle construction, so much so that Moses orders them to stop.

The skilled craftsmen have more than enough supplies required to assemble the tabernacle. Through God's appointment, Moses calls Bezalel and Oholiab to lead the project. The Lord fills them and the other craftsmen with His Spirit, endowing them with artistic ability. God's Spirit gifts them with wisdom, understanding, and aptitude so that they can accomplish the work excellently. Moses oversees as Bezalel and Oholiab gather the materials for the tabernacle. A place of beauty, the tabernacle would be a picture of God's throne room in heaven. The craftsmen would also create clothing for the priests who were chosen to steward the tabernacle and lead the Israelites in right worship. Their clothing would be ornate and royal. God selects Aaron and his sons to serve as priests in the tabernacle (Exodus 28:1). There, the priests are to perform animal sacrifices or worship rituals to atone for the people's sins and represent the nation of Israel before God. Through their priestly duties, the glory of the Lord would remain in the Holy of Holies, the innermost part of the tabernacle. Here, the invisible God would rest, and the people would be blessed by His presence among them.

In today's passage, we see the restoration of the covenant bond between God and the Israelites. Through Moses's intercession and the worship duties of the priests later, God will continue to be their God and abide with them in the tabernacle. Unfortunately, communion in the tabernacle would not last. The Israelites' grateful hearts seen in Exodus 35 would once again turn idolatrous later in redemptive history. Complete restoration of our covenant relationship with God is only accomplished through the intercession of the true High Priest, Jesus. He has done so by loving the Father and keeping His commands. Through His sacrifice, He makes a bridge between us and God. Jesus repairs the relationship our idolatry violated. When we place our faith in Him and His saving work, Jesus brings us into permanent Sabbath rest where we are forever grateful for the Spirit of God who dwells with us.

11

JESUS REPAIRS THE RELATIONSHIP
OUR IDOLATRY VIOLATED.

How does keeping the Sabbath rest protect the Israelites from falling into idolatry again?

_____

_____

_____

_____

_____

_____

_____

As seen in today's reading, thankful hearts lead to generosity in worship. How do you show gratitude for the Lord's saving work? Where can you be more generous?

_____

_____

_____

_____

_____

_____

_____

How does Spirit-given creative ability in the construction of the tabernacle affect how you view the various gifts among the church body? How does this show our dependence on God for all things?

_____

_____

_____

_____

_____

_____

_____

"GOD, NOW THROUGH MOSES, IS AGAIN ESTABLISHING HIS HOLY KINGDOM AND DWELLING PLACE ON EARTH."

WEEK 5 / DAY 4

Building the Tabernacle

Though the craftsmen prepare the parts, it is Moses himself who will assemble the tabernacle. Scholars point out the similarities between the creation account in Genesis chapters 1 and 2 and the construction of the tabernacle. Moses echoes God's creative work when He formed the universe. At that time, God established the garden of Eden as His sacred space where He would dwell with mankind. Faithful to His covenant commitment, God, now through Moses, is again establishing His holy kingdom and dwelling place on earth.

Moses begins with assembling the Holy of Holies, the innermost part of the tabernacle. Moses installs the ark of the covenant, a gold-covered wooden chest. Inside the chest, he puts the Ten Commandments and a jar of manna. The Ten Commandments represent the Lord's enduring words, and the manna represents His divine provision. He places the mercy seat on the ark of the covenant. The golden mercy seat has sculptures of two cherubim facing each other. The cherubim are angelic beings with golden wings to cover themselves and the area between them. The glory of the invisible God would reside between the cherubim. The ark of the covenant and the mercy seat mirror the Lord's heavenly throne. In front of the ark, Moses raises a curtain that has designs of angelic beings, marking the separation between spaces and showing a reverence for God's most sacred area.

Moses then assembles the Holy Place where the priests would perform daily worship rituals. On one side, he places a gold-covered, wooden table for the bread of the Presence. The table for the bread of the Presence would have twelve loaves of bread on it to represent the twelve tribes of Israel. On the opposite side, he brings in a solid gold lampstand and assembles its seven lights. The lampstand would provide light to the priests as they complete their duties. Its seven lights also symbolize completion and wholeness. Directly in front of the curtain to the Holy of Holies, Moses places a gold-covered, wooden altar for incense. He burns the fragrant incense on the altar which would emit before the Lord's presence in the Holy of Holies. The incense represents the prayers of the people and conveys that they are like a pleasing aroma before God. Moses puts up the screen for the entrance and lays four coverings over the Holy Place and the Holy of Holies.

Outside the tent entrance, Moses sets up the courtyard. He brings a bronze altar for animal sacrifices and a bronze basin filled with water for ceremonial washing. The altar would burn with hot coals to represent the judgment of God. There, the people would also offer a grain offering as a gift for the Lord. At the basin, the priests would need to wash before and after their duties. This action symbolizes the need to be cleansed from the impurity of sin. Next, Moses takes oil and anoints every part of the tabernacle. Like God blessing His creative work in Genesis chapters 1 and 2, Moses blesses the tabernacle and makes it holy, or set apart for the Lord's glory. Moses also anoints Aaron and his sons for the priesthood and clothes them with the holy garments. He inaugurates their permanent priesthood, a sign that God is committed to making the people His own possession (Exodus 19:5-6).

When Moses finishes, a thick cloud descends and covers the area. In all His majesty and splendor, the glory of God fills the tabernacle. He is no longer hidden by a pillar of cloud or fire. God is fully revealed in the Holy of Holies. But, Moses is unable to enter. Entering the awe-inspiring presence of God still requires just payment for sin. Only the priests can enter the Holy of Holies one day of the year after adhering to specific worship standards. Moses is so close to the fullness of God, but his sin still keeps him far away, preventing complete intimacy with his Creator. Though the tabernacle is a remembrance of the garden of Eden, it has limitations. But, the tabernacle also points to a future hope. Moses remembers God's redemptive promise to Adam and Eve and looks forward to the Son who will come to establish God's true kingdom and will fully restore all things to Himself.

Even though Moses was the chosen deliverer, he was still not able to enter into the full presence of God. Moses looked to the true High Priest who would accomplish what the tabernacle represented. Jesus is this true High Priest, fully God and fully man, who is the perfect sacrificial grain and incense offering before the Lord. Like the twelve loaves of bread in the tabernacle, He is our representative who gives us His righteousness. Shown through the basin for ceremonial washing, He is the only one who is completely pure and without sin. Seen in the Holy of Holies, Jesus is the fulfillment of God's law. He is our Bread of Life. And He possesses the fullness of God. His death ripped the curtain in two, and by His blood, we can enter the holiness of God without hesitation.

MOSES LOOKED TO THE TRUE HIGH PRIEST WHO WOULD ACCOMPLISH WHAT THE TABERNACLE REPRESENTED.

Read Hebrews 8:1-6. Why was it important for Moses to follow the Lord's instructions for the tabernacle exactly?

Read Colossians 1:19-20 and Hebrews 10:19-22. How do you respond knowing that you can only enter God's holy presence through the saving work of Jesus?

In what specific ways can you exercise more boldness as a redeemed child of God?

The
Tabernacle

W

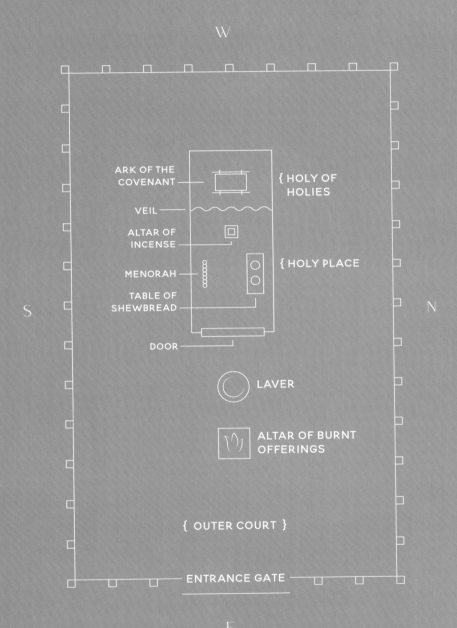

ARK OF THE
COVENANT

{ HOLY OF
HOLIES

VEIL

ALTAR OF
INCENSE

{ HOLY PLACE

MENORAH

TABLE OF
SHEWBREAD

S   N

DOOR

LAVER

ALTAR OF BURNT
OFFERINGS

{ OUTER COURT }

ENTRANCE GATE

E

"BY GOD'S GRACE THROUGH FAITH IN JESUS, THE BLOOD OF THE TRUE HIGH PRIEST CONTINUES TO COVER OUR SINS."

WEEK 5 / DAY 5

Dwelling Among Us

This week, we observed that God comes near to His people despite their unfaithfulness. Because of his sinful nature, Moses could not fully draw near to God in the tabernacle. In today's John and Matthew passages, we see not only how Jesus is the physical embodiment of the tabernacle but also how His saving work has erased the separation between the Holy of Holies and believers, making the intimate presence of God always near.

In chapter 1 verses 1-18, the disciple John writes a prologue to begin his account of Jesus's life. This preface focuses on the divine nature of Jesus. John writes, "In the beginning was the Word, and the Word was with God, and the Word was God" (John 1:1). Jesus is the Word of God, eternally existing with the Father and the Holy Spirit. Jesus was active in the creation of the universe and continues to hold all things together by His agency and power. John then introduces Jesus's mission. As Creator of the universe, Jesus has brought life to the world and exposed the darkness of sin with His light. Those who believe in Him have become children of God and are invited into a covenant relationship with Him. The gift of adoption into the family of God was made possible only through His sending His Son to the world to die in our place. John then states, "The Word became flesh and dwelt among us" (John 1:14). The literal translation for the Greek word used for "dwelt" is "tabernacled or dwelt in a tent." John is referencing the tabernacle structure during the wilderness journey in Exodus to describe His coming. Like God filling the tabernacle to reconcile the Israelites, Jesus, fully God, took on a tent of flesh and reconciled those who believe in the covenant promises made to Abraham. The restoration through the tabernacle was a picture of the true restoration that the Son of God has brought. Jesus is Immanuel or God with us (Matthew 1:23). On the outside, the tabernacle was not visually appealing, but on the inside, there was much beauty and wonder from the Lord's divine presence. Similarly, as Isaiah 53:2 says, Jesus "didn't have an impressive form or majesty that we should look at him, no appearance that we should desire him." But, within Him, the fullness of God was pleased to dwell. He revealed the beauty and glory of the Father and made us recipients of divine grace.

In John 2, Jesus proclaims He is the true tabernacle. At this point in redemptive history, the people of God are no longer journeying through the wilderness. Therefore, a stationary temple has replaced the portable tabernacle as the place of worship. The temple resides in the city of Jerusalem, and in this passage, the people of God are traveling there to celebrate Passover, the time when the Lord brought the Israelites out of Egypt. Jesus approaches the temple and sees a marketplace there. Instead of worshiping God and remembering His faithfulness and mercy, the people are buying and selling goods for profit. Jesus has righteous anger toward their irreverence of His "Father's house" (John 2:16). He drives them out with passion, fulfilling the prophecy in Malachi 3:1-4. But the people demand a sign to prove that Jesus has the authority to evict businesses from the temple. Jesus responds, "Destroy this temple, and I will raise it up in three days" (John 2:19). Jesus predicts that the people would ruin the temple, but by His authority, He will raise it up again. Here, Jesus is associating the temple with his own body. The sin of the people would drive Jesus to the cross and the grave, but He would be resurrected three days later, showing the ultimate sign of His divine authority.

Our sin brought ruin upon His body. His flesh was wrecked like temple brick or tabernacle covering falling to the ground from enemy plunder. But while suffering on the cross, He looked upon us with grace and mercy. His plan to dwell amongst His people was not forfeited. His death was the means through which our debt was paid, judgment satisfied, and our souls restored to wholeness. His death ensured that the presence of God would be among His people forever. Matthew 27:50-51 states that when Jesus breathed His last, the curtain in front of the Holy of Holies was torn from top to bottom. Through His sacrifice, the barrier between God and His people was severed. In this way, Jesus is also the true High Priest who represented our sin and offered Himself to take punishment. By God's grace through faith in Jesus, the blood of the true High Priest continues to cover our sins. He has led us into right worship and completely restored our relationship with the Father. Also, at His ascension to the heavenly throne, He sent the Holy Spirit to dwell inside us, making us His living tabernacles. We can forever rest in the eternal presence of God.

AT HIS ASCENSION TO THE HEAVENLY THRONE, HE SENT THE HOLY SPIRIT TO DWELL INSIDE US, MAKING US HIS LIVING TABERNACLES.

Read Hebrews 9. How does God fulfill His commitment to establishing a permanent priesthood (Exodus 19:5-6)?

_____

_____

_____

_____

_____

_____

_____

As the tabernacle, or temple of God, how can you represent His light and life to the world?

_____

_____

_____

_____

_____

_____

Spend a moment resting in God's presence, and write a prayer of thankfulness for His nearness.

_____

_____

_____

_____

_____

_____

_____

LISTEN TO THE HYMN, "HE HIDETH MY SOUL," AND MEDI-
TATE ON THE LYRICS BELOW.

HE HIDETH MY SOUL IN THE CLEFT OF THE ROCK
THAT SHADOWS A DRY, THIRSTY LAND;
HE HIDETH MY LIFE IN THE DEPTHS OF HIS LOVE,
AND COVERS ME THERE WITH HIS HAND,
AND COVERS ME THERE WITH HIS HAND.

Fanny Crosby
"He Hideth My Soul"
1890

I PRAY THAT HE MAY GRANT
YOU, ACCORDING TO THE
RICHES OF HIS GLORY,
TO BE STRENGTHENED
WITH POWER IN YOUR INNER
BEING THROUGH HIS SPIRIT,
AND THAT CHRIST MAY
DWELL IN YOUR
HEARTS THROUGH FAITH.

Ephesians 3:16-17a

Week 05 Reflection

Summarize the main points from this week's Scripture readings.

_____

_____

_____

_____

_____

_____

_____

_____

_____

_____

_____

_____

What did you observe from this week's passages about God and His character?

_____

_____

_____

_____

_____

_____

_____

_____

_____

_____

_____

_____

What do this week's passages reveal about the condition of mankind and yourself?

_____

_____

_____

_____

_____

_____

_____

How do these passages point to the gospel?

_____

_____

_____

_____

_____

How should you respond to these Scriptures? What specific action steps can you take this week to apply them in your life?

_____

_____

_____

_____

_____

_____

_____

_____

_____

Write a prayer in response to your study of God's Word. Adore God for who He is, confess sins that He revealed in your own life, ask Him to empower you to walk in obedience, and pray for anyone who comes to mind as you study.

_____

_____

_____

_____

_____

_____

_____

_____

_____

Leadership Deficiencies

"THE INTERCESSION OF THE FAITHFUL MEDIATOR IS NECESSARY TO COVER THE PEOPLE'S UNBELIEF."

WEEK 6 / DAY 1

Joining in Grumbling

With the new tabernacle packed up, the Israelites set off from the Wilderness of Sinai and continue their journey to the Promised Land. God in the pillar of cloud and the ark of the covenant travel ahead of them. The Israelites begin a three-day journey through the wilderness. It could not have been an easy feat traveling through the tough terrain. Though their God is right in front of them, the Israelites complain without discretion. The people have gotten too comfortable in their relationship with the Lord; they grumble openly without reverence for Him. They have quickly forgotten His loving-kindness shown through His presence in the tabernacle. Then, at the Israelite camp, the people gather together, and the complaining grows, revealing their unbelief. The Lord sees their lack of faith, and His righteous anger burns against them. He sends fire to the outskirts of their camp, perhaps to wake them out of their delusion. God could have justly brought fire to the entire camp. Instead, He shows His patience and rouses Moses to pray on their behalf. Through this intercession, God displays His mercy. The intercession of the faithful mediator is necessary to cover the people's unbelief.

One morning, the people go out into the field to collect the manna the Lord has provided for them. As seen in Exodus 16, the manna is a wafer-like substance that appears after the morning dew dries. Manna is pounded, shaped, and boiled to make the bread of heaven. Scripture describes the bread like a "pastry cooked with the finest oil" (Numbers 11:8). It is no ordinary food but a sweet and heavenly cake fit for the angels. But it seems that collecting and preparing the manna has become mundane to the Israelites. They have grown tired of its taste, just as their taste, or desire, for the Lord seems to have changed as well. Their relationship with the Lord appears to have become a mundane experience for them. The riffraff among the Israelites, people of other ethnicities from Egypt, are the first to make complaints (Numbers 11:4). Complaining is contagious, and soon, the Israelites join the grumbling. They cried, "Who will feed us meat? We remember the fresh fish we ate in Egypt, along with the cucumber, melon, leeks, onions, and garlic. But now, our appetite is gone; there's nothing to look at but this manna!" (Numbers 11:4-6). Family after family comes to Moses with their demands and weeping. After all this time, the complaints become too much for Moses. Moses himself, the chosen mediator, is now swept up in their grumbling. He complains to the Lord, "Why have you brought such trouble on your servant? Why are you angry with me, and why do you burden me with all these people?" Moses decides that they are too much for him to handle. He concludes that if God is going to treat him like this, then He should just go ahead and kill him now.

God responds with grace to Moses's rash behavior. He anoints seventy men who can help carry the weight Moses is feeling. The Spirit of the Lord rests on them. The men begin to prophesy—declaring truth, exposing sin, and pointing the Israelites back to God. With these new leaders appointed, Joshua, Moses's assistant, seems to feel that Moses's leadership as the sole intercessor is being threatened. But, Moses, knowing His limitations, accepts the change. God graciously supplies the help Moses needs, even though Moses does not intercede for the people after their food demands. Instead of praying for the Israelites, Moses joins their grumbling. To address the people's complaints, the Lord declares He will send them meat to eat for a month. He will give them over to the sinful desires of their heart. The Israelites will eat so much meat that it will consequently make them sick. Getting what they want leads to judgment. The people gather and eat the abundance of quail that the Lord sends them. Gluttonous, the Israelites devour the meat day and night. The Lord sees their unbelief and ingratitude, and His just anger burns again. This time, Moses is silent. While they are feasting, the Lord sends a plague to them and allows them to get severely sick in their overconsumption of meat, and the people are left to face the result of their sin.

In today's passage, we see Moses weaken in his role as a mediator. Though Moses grumbled, the Lord extended grace to him. The Lord covered his sin with the intercession of the true Mediator to come. By the grace of God, though his faith was weak, Moses still looked forward to the promised Messiah, the Priest-King, who would truly intercede by sacrificing Himself. Jesus is the true Mediator, and on the cross, Jesus died for Moses's grumbling. Through Jesus's saving work, Moses received God's favor. Likewise, Jesus died for our complaining and unbelief. During His life, Jesus's obedience and faithfulness earned for us the gift of grace. We receive the Holy Spirit who gives us the faith to overcome our unbelief. The indwelling Holy Spirit keeps us from consuming the concerns of this world which lead to our destruction and instead helps us to feast on the greater pleasure of eternity with Jesus.

JESUS DIED FOR OUR COMPLAINING AND UNBELIEF.

When has complaining in a situation revealed your lack of faith in God?

_____

_____

_____

_____

_____

_____

_____

_____

When do your affections for the Lord turn dull? How can you strive toward a deeper faith in these moments?

_____

_____

_____

_____

_____

_____

_____

Read 1 Timothy 2:1-4. In what areas can you intercede, or pray for others?

_____

_____

_____

_____

_____

_____

_____

"SCOUTING THE LAND ASSURES THEM THE REST IS SOON TO COME."

WEEK 6 / DAY 2

Scouting the Land

In the Wilderness of Paran, God tells Moses to choose a leader from each tribe of Israel and have them scout out the land of Canaan. Each man will represent their ancestral clan as if the whole nation of Israel itself is getting a glimpse of the long-awaited Promised Land. The men are to gather details and give an objective report on the demographics and geography. They are also to bring some fruit back from the land to prove its agricultural condition. God does not send the leaders on this task to learn about the land for Himself. All-knowing, God could have easily relayed information about Canaan to Moses and the Israelites. However, through this mission, God invites the people to get a taste of the bounteous land that He promised them. God graciously allows the Israelites to renew their hope. Scouting the land assures them the rest is soon to come. The men are unaware and fearful of what they will discover in Canaan. Moses calls them to "Be courageous" (Numbers 13:20). They must scout out the land with faith and trust in God.

The men survey the whole area of Canaan. They make their way into Hebron, a city in the region, where the Anakim are living. Anakim people are giants and strong warriors. The men then move ahead to the Valley of Eshcol. The men see clusters of large grapes hanging off branches. They cut down a single cluster that is so huge that it needs to be carried on a pole by two men. They also take some pomegranates and figs. Canaan is truly "a land flowing with milk and honey" (Numbers 13:27). This phrase refers to the land's fertility, richness, and desirability. The men see that the Lord's word is true.

When they return to the Wilderness of Paran, the scouts report what they saw and deliver the fruit to Moses and the community. After relaying the information, Caleb and Joshua, two of the scouts, are ready to claim the land as they are sure the Lord will help them obtain it. But the other men are too fearful of the Anakim. They believe the Israelites are at a disadvantage and will be destroyed. These men lack faith in God to fulfill His word in giving them the Promised Land. The rest of the Israelites also respond in fear to the news. They cry that they would rather die in the wilderness or return to Egypt. The people's weeping escalates to rage as they threaten to stone Moses and Aaron.

Amid the intensity, God speaks to Moses. He says, "How long will these people despise me?" (Numbers 14:11). God mourns their unbelief. The Lord tells Moses He will do away with them and create a new nation through Moses. God is longsuffering and just. The Lord does not desire anyone to perish. But He will also punish the wicked and reward the faithful. Fortunately, Moses is not silent this time. The Lord's threat of judgment rouses Moses to intercede on behalf of the Israelites. Moses intercedes by reminding the Lord of His commitment to His glory. He tells God that His glorious reputation would be tarnished if He does not bring them to the Promised Land. Based on the Lord's character, Moses asks God to pardon the people's sin. The Lord then grants this request. To preserve His glory, the Lord will not destroy them. He will continue to use rebellious people in His sovereign will until His covenant promises are fulfilled for His name's sake. However, God does not let the guilty go unpunished. He will honor the Israelites' desire to die in the wilderness rather than rest in the Promised Land. Like in yesterday's passage, their rebellious desires lead to judgment. The generation of people who complained and longed for death rather than life will die in the wilderness. But, Caleb, Joshua, and the others who held onto their faith in God will receive the gift of life and rest in God's Holy Land.

In today's passages, we see God's faithful, merciful, and just character as a commitment to His glory. Holding His honor as the utmost reason, God pursued and preserved the Israelites from being consumed by their sin. Through Jesus's mediation, we see God's glory on full display. Jesus's death on the cross shows that God was faithful to His covenant promises in sending His Son to establish His people and kingdom. Jesus took our punishment for sin, satisfying divine justice. God extends us mercy, as we do not receive the eternal separation from God that we deserve. Jesus accomplished our salvation for God's glory. Through Christ, God made a way for us to come to Himself. There, in His presence, we experience the grace of utmost peace and satisfaction. The source of true rest and life is God's glorious character and His commitment to His own name. Let us point to God's glory by trusting in and living in the saving work of Jesus.

CALEB, JOSHUA, AND THE OTHERS WHO HELD ONTO THEIR FAITH IN GOD WILL RECEIVE THE GIFT OF LIFE AND REST IN GOD'S HOLY LAND.

In Numbers 14:39-45, when the Israelites attempt to claim the Promised Land on their own, they are driven back by the Canaanites they had originally feared. What does this event reveal about the placement of their faith? What is the result of misplaced faith?

_____

_____

_____

_____

_____

_____

When has God allowed you to follow the sinful desires of your heart? What were the consequences?

_____

_____

_____

_____

_____

_____

Read Isaiah 48:9-11. How do you respond to God's commitment to His glory and its revelation in Jesus?

_____

_____

_____

_____

_____

_____

"THE ISRAELITES FINALLY REALIZE THEIR SINFULNESS AND INABILITY TO APPROACH GOD ON THEIR OWN."

WEEK 6 / DAY 3

Between the Living and the Dead

The air among the Israelites remains tense after their reluctance to travel into the Promised Land. They have grown tired of the wilderness and tired of Moses and Aaron's leadership. They want to know why Moses gets all the power and why Aaron's sons are the only ones allowed in the Holy Place? Pride and discontentment in their hearts manifest outwardly. Korah, a man from the tribe of Kohath, gathers 250 men and confronts Moses and Aaron. They demand an open-door policy for the tabernacle. They declare everyone is holy and can enter the sanctity of the tabernacle. Moses calls for Korah and his men to realize the blessing God has already given them. The Lord has commissioned the Kohathites to carry the materials of the tabernacle. They can draw near to the Lord's holiness more than most. Korah and the crowd also misunderstand the priesthood. Aaron and his sons do not enter the tabernacle because they are more holy. They have to perform sacrifices and cleansing rituals to atone and purify themselves of their sin before they can carry on with their priestly duties. The Lord has anointed roles in worship unto Him, but all of the Israelites are steeped in sin and need God's grace.

Moses is grieved by the rebellion. He presents a way to prove who God's chosen leaders are. Moses tells Korah and his followers to prepare firepans with incense and offer them before the Lord the next morning. Aaron will do the same. Moses knows the Lord will settle this dispute Himself. Moses tries to dissuade two men, Dathan and Abiram, from following Korah and urges them to come to the Lord's side. Resisting, they say, "We will not come! Is it not enough that you brought us up from a land flowing with milk and honey to kill us in the wilderness?" (Numbers 16:12-13). Dathan and Abiram view Egypt as a truly rich and desirable land. They exchange God's truth for Satan's lie. They would rather take a fool's paradise than God's sure promise. Moses becomes angry at their irreverence.

When morning arrives the next day, Korah and the entire community face Moses and Aaron at the entrance to the tabernacle. Then the glory of the Lord appears. Korah and his followers witness the Lord's awe-inspiring glory. The holiness of God causes them to tremble. But they have received what they wanted. Again, their desires lead to judgment. Sinners cannot be in the presence of the Holy God without an intercessor, or God's power will overtake them. The Lord tells Moses and Aaron to separate themselves from the community, for His holiness will consume the people. Moses and Aaron fall face down and plead for the Lord's mercy, and God grants it. The Lord protects the Israelites from His judgment, but Korah and his original band are consumed by earth and fire. The next day, the saved Israelites do not express gratitude but complain. Hard-hearted, they claim that Moses and Aaron have killed the Lord's people. The people have not learned anything from yesterday's catastrophe. But, Moses and Aaron still intercede to save them from being consumed by the Lord's glory. They work quickly. Aaron grabs his incense offering and makes atonement for the people. Aaron stands "between the dead and the living" (Numbers 16:48). Representing the people, Aaron makes a payment for their sin and satisfies the divine judgment. He halts the death that the people brought upon themselves through their rebellion and gives them life in a relationship with God.

This new life is represented in Aaron's staff. The Lord calls for a staff from each of the twelve tribes to be placed in the tabernacle. The next day, Moses enters the tabernacle to retrieve them and marvels at Aaron's staff. Aaron's staff has sprouted, bloomed flowers, and produced almonds. The staff made of dead wood is now like the branch of an almond tree. The rest of the staffs remain without life. This miracle proves Aaron and his lineage are the anointed priesthood, and through their worship, they will bring the people into fruitfulness. At this moment, the Israelites finally realize their sinfulness and inability to approach God on their own. They must depend on God's provision through the chosen priest to have abundant life.

In today's reading, we see the Israelites follow their desires to death. But through Moses's intercession and Aaron's atonement, the people are brought back into life and relationship with God. Moses and Aaron are sinners as well. But their actions point to the true High Priest who perfectly intercedes and atones for all of God's people. Their roles have their fulfillment in Jesus Christ. Through the Israelites' cry at the end of chapter 17, we see that we too are lost if we do not depend on the chosen High Priest. We will remain like dead wood if we do not seek Jesus who is like a tree planted by the streams of living water and never withers. He conquered death in His resurrection, and when we believe in Him, the resurrecting power of the Holy Spirit will also raise us into eternal life with God.

WE TOO ARE LOST IF WE DO NOT DEPEND ON THE CHOSEN HIGH PRIEST.

When have you sought to worship by your standards and efforts rather than God's?

_____

_____

_____

_____

_____

_____

_____

_____

The fire pan and Aaron's staff were kept in the tabernacle as signs. What do they reveal about God's character?

_____

_____

_____

_____

_____

_____

_____

Read Ephesians 2:1-10. In what areas has your life bloomed like Aaron's staff because of the life-giving power of salvation through Jesus?

_____

_____

_____

_____

_____

_____

_____

"GOD GRACIOUSLY
OFFERS A WAY
FOR THE PEOPLE
TO EXERCISE THEIR
WEAK FAITH AND
RECEIVE HEALING."

WEEK 6 / DAY 4

Raising the Bronze Snake

The sign of Aaron's staff confirming his priesthood does not satisfy the Israelites for long. Because of the desert condition, they raise their voices to ask to return to Egypt or perish. Because of their unbelief in response to the negative report on the Promised Land, the Israelites will now have to wander a total of forty years until the older generation who lacked faith dies (Numbers 14:33). The Israelites do not realize their sin has further extended and worsened their journey. But, God allows the additional time to grow the Israelites' faith and show more of His character. The Lord protects and sustains His people, as the Promised Land is still on the horizon.

To alleviate their thirst, God tells Moses and Aaron to take the staff and speak to the rock while everyone is watching. The rock will yield water for the people. Moses and Aaron are to only speak to the rock, but they disregard this command. After hearing complaint after complaint, the men are full of seeming resentment and frustration toward the community. "Listen, you rebels!" Moses shouts (Numbers 20:10). Scholars point out that Moses inappropriately takes the role of a judge here, replaying the issue of pride he had as a prince in Egypt. The old Moses who took matters into his own hands and killed the Egyptian man is back. Moses and Aaron assume their authority, and Moses strikes the rock with his staff twice. Water pours out for the people. However, Moses and Aaron are no heroes here, but rebels, becoming what they called the Israelites. Disappointed in their disobedience, the Lord tells them that because of their lack of faith, they too will not enter the Promised Land.

Moses's resentful heart further lures him away from God. Scholars argue that his quick move to the region of Edom suggests that Moses continues in disobedience. God does not give him the command to go to Edom, but Moses takes this direction on his own. But, the king of Edom does not allow passage and threatens attack if they try. Moses is not successful as a commander here. Edom's armed forces come out to defend their land, and the Israelites turn away. After this failure, Moses likely realizes he cannot complete the mission on his own. He must return to the Lord, trust in Him, and heed His word. By God's grace, Moses's faith is strengthened, and he adheres to the Lord's command to instate Eleazar, Aaron's son, as the next priest. On Mount Hor at the edge of Edom, Moses takes Aaron's priestly garments and gives them to Eleazar. Aaron receives the consequence of his sin, but God is merciful. The priesthood will continue through Aaron's lineage, and Aaron dies on the mountain, surely with gratitude and hope that the true High Priest will one day come, and He will be perfectly faithful and obedient.

Moses leads the people toward Canaan by the Lord's direction. When the king of Arad confronts them, they ask the Lord for His help, and He gives them victory. Scholars claim that total destruction of the enemy nation shows that God is fulfilling His covenant promise and using the Israelites to exercise judgment on evil nations. This battle points forward to the eternal dwelling place that all faithful believers will receive when the Lord defeats evil for good and reclaims His world from Satan's grip.

Even after this great victory, the Israelites desperately want to return to oppressive slavery in Egypt and die under Pharaoh's harsh rule. The Lord sends snakes to the people, and many die from the poisonous bites. The Lord is not being cruel here, but the Israelites suffer the consequence of their sin. Scholars argue that snakes are a representation of Egypt and Satan himself. In this way, by sending the snakes, God gives the people what they desire most: a return to bondage, pain, and death. However, God graciously offers a way for the people to exercise their weak faith and receive healing. Moses intercedes and, upon the Lord's command, raises a mounted bronze snake on a pole. The mounted bronze serpent shows that evil has been seized by divine power. Whoever looks at the risen snake is healed from the snake's bite. The pole does not have any supernatural ability; God Himself restores the people. But looking at the bronze serpent is a symbol of the Israelites placing their small faith in God to defeat evil and make them whole again.

By God's grace, Moses returned to be a faithful mediator and raised the bronze snake for the people's salvation. The bronze serpent pointed to true salvation in Jesus. Bit by the serpent at His heel, Jesus suffered the divine judgment we deserved. In John 3:14, Jesus states, "Just as Moses lifted up the snake in the wilderness, so the Son of Man must be lifted up." Like the cursed serpent on the pole, Jesus was raised on the cross, becoming sin so that He could redeem us (2 Corinthians 5:21). By His death and resurrection, Jesus crushed the serpent's head, ultimately defeating Satan and spiritual evil. When He rose from the grave, He rose in divine glory with the conquered serpent in His hands. Look to Jesus, for He is the risen Lord who saves us from death in the wilderness and gives us eternal life.

LOOK TO JESUS, FOR HE IS THE RISEN LORD WHO SAVES US FROM DEATH IN THE WILDERNESS AND GIVES US ETERNAL LIFE.

Where have your priorities shown a desire for counterfeit pleasures instead of life with God?

_____

_____

_____

_____

_____

_____

_____

How have your past struggles shown themselves on your current faith journey? How does Jesus restore these moments?

_____

_____

_____

_____

_____

_____

Faith in Jesus is the requirement for peace and abiding with God. Write a prayer for your faith to be strengthened and for the Holy Spirit to help you look to the risen Savior in times of weakness.

_____

_____

_____

_____

_____

_____

_____

"MOSES AND AARON HOPED IN ONE WHO COULD LEAD GOD'S PEOPLE WITHOUT FALLING INTO SIN HIMSELF."

Sinless in the Face of Persecution

Despite their faithfulness and obedience, Moses and Aaron sinned, too. Their faults made apparent the need for a true priest, prophet, and deliverer. Moses and Aaron hoped in One who could lead God's people without falling into sin Himself. He would always be patient, long-suffering, just, merciful, and loving. He would face the darkness of sin and carry its burdens humbly. He would intercede to prevent rebellious hearts from wandering into death and set them on the course to life and rest with God. Such perfection could only be seen in God Himself. God would have to come to be the true Priest, Prophet, and Deliverer for His people. God accomplished His plan of redemption in the person of Jesus Christ. Jesus is the one sent from heaven, the perfect Son of God, who restores our relationship with God the Father.

In the first reading, Jesus is confronted by a large mob. From chief priests to elders, the people are carrying swords and clubs. Their hearts are full of rage. Believing Jesus to be a blasphemer, the people are here to put an end to Jesus's ministry. Judas, one of Jesus's disciples, is leading them. He greets Jesus with a kiss on the cheek, a sign of salutation at the time. But this sign also identifies Jesus as the one the mob is looking for. Though knowing Judas has let their location be known in exchange for financial reward, Jesus calls him "friend" (Matthew 26:50). Unlike Moses, Jesus holds the moral authority to judge. However, Jesus does not condemn Judas. Instead, He opens Himself to receive Judas's stinging embrace: a sweet kiss dripping with greed and contempt. Immediately, they arrest Jesus. Peter, another disciple, attacks a man in the crowd. Jesus tells Peter to put up his sword. It is not the time for fighting; it is the time for saving. Jesus has the power to escape the suffering that awaits Him, but He remains obedient to His Father's plan. Then, His disciples scatter, and He is left alone with evil. Jesus is led away to the high priest to stand on trial. Jesus remains meek and calm while others are bearing false witness against Him. He receives the accusations, abuse, and mocking without uttering a word of malice toward the people. Amidst the shouting and insults, a rooster crows. signifying that Jesus's words about Peter have been fulfilled. Peter was the disciple who was the most zealous for Jesus to reign as Messiah, the Anointed One who would deliver God's people. But now, Peter has denied knowing Jesus three times in fear that he too will be arrested. Jesus is the suffering servant who is rejected by even His closest confidant.

In Matthew 27, the people demand Jesus's death. It is decided that He will die by crucifixion, criminal punishment under the Roman government. The Roman soldiers gather around Jesus and strip Him of His clothes. They give Jesus a scarlet robe, crown of thorns, and a staff. They spit on Him and beat His head. After the derision, the soldiers lead Him away to the place of judgment. They mount Jesus on the cross, nailing His hands and feet into the splintering wood. The soldiers raise the cross in the sky, situating it between two other crucifixions. Jesus hangs there, innocent, between two criminals. He hears temptation from Satan. He hears scathing commands to save Himself from the pain and humiliation. But, instead of giving in to Satan's trap, Jesus intercedes on behalf of the people and trusts God that through suffering, there will be life. Jesus prays for His enemies saying, "Father, forgive them, because they do not know what they are doing" (Luke 23:34). While the people are laughing at His body being torn apart, Jesus is praying for God to show them mercy. This is the ultimate intercession. Moses showed us a picture of the mediator role; unfortunately, he was not able to withstand grumbling from the Israelites. But, Jesus bears the unbearable and suffers unto death to atone for His abusers' sin and reconcile them to God.

Our sins put us in the mob, the crowd that cheered for Jesus's crucifixion. In our fallenness, we too rejected Jesus. Like Peter, we feared the opinions of men and viewed our reputation as more worthy to defend than the gospel. Like Judas, we traded a satisfying and life-giving relationship with Jesus for counterfeit pleasures of this world. In our unbelief, we did not understand the cross is the accomplishment of God's glorious plan of redemption and the display of His love for us. But, praise be to God that His love for us was stronger than our sin. Through Jesus's saving work, we can look to the cross for forgiveness and eternal life (John 3:15). Jesus was lifted up in shame on the cross so that we would be lifted up in His righteousness. We are restored to God, and one day, we will resurrect like our Savior who rose from the grave in glorious victory over evil. Gaze upon and cling to the cross of Christ; it is light and truth for the world (John 3:19-21).

JESUS BEARS THE UNBEARABLE AND SUFFERS
UNTO DEATH TO ATONE FOR HIS ABUSERS' SIN
AND RECONCILE THEM TO GOD.

Explain how persevering through trials for the gospel reflects God's longsuffering character.

How can you grow in boldness when sharing faith with others?

Read Matthew 5:43-48. Write a prayer for the salvation of those who have done you harm.

TODAY:

DRAW A PICTURE INSPIRED BY THE THEMES OF
SUFFERING AND PERSEVERANCE.

SCRIPTURE MEMORY

06

FOR THE WORD OF THE CROSS IS FOOLISHNESS TO THOSE WHO ARE PERISHING, BUT IT IS THE POWER OF GOD TO US WHO ARE BEING SAVED.

1 Corinthians 1:18

Week 06 Reflection

{ REVIEW ALL PASSAGES FROM THE WEEK }

Summarize the main points from this week's Scripture readings.

_____
_____
_____
_____
_____
_____
_____
_____
_____
_____
_____

What did you observe from this week's passages about God and His character?

_____
_____
_____
_____
_____
_____
_____
_____
_____
_____
_____

What do this week's passages reveal about the condition of mankind and yourself?

_____
_____
_____
_____
_____
_____
_____

How do these passages point to the gospel?

_____

_____

_____

_____

_____

_____

How should you respond to these Scriptures? What specific action steps can you take this week to apply them in your life?

_____

_____

_____

_____

_____

_____

_____

Write a prayer in response to your study of God's Word. Adore God for who He is, confess sins that He revealed in your own life, ask Him to empower you to walk in obedience, and pray for anyone who comes to mind as you study.

_____

_____

_____

_____

_____

_____

_____

A Call to Love & Obey

"TO ENJOY THE
BLESSING OF
GOD'S HOLY LAND
AND PRESENCE,
THE ISRAELITES
MUST RESPOND TO
THE LORD'S LOVE
IN OBEDIENCE,
WORSHIP, AND
GRATITUDE."

WEEK 7 / DAY 1

Responding to the Lord's Love

Now in the fortieth year in the wilderness, Moses and the Israelites stand across from the Jordan River. After battling and overcoming the pagan kings of the region in Numbers, they have reached the end of their journey and are at the precipice of the Promised Land. Because of his disobedience at the rock in Numbers 20, Moses cannot enter Canaan with the people, and his death is approaching, but God calls him to relay last words of encouragement, advice, and warning. Moses recounts how the Lord has protected them from their enemies and carried them to this point. But as Moses explains in this chapter of Deuteronomy, to enjoy the blessing of God's Holy Land and presence, the Israelites must respond to the Lord's love in obedience, worship, and gratitude.

Moses calls the people to listen to the law of God. Such adherence to these statutes will result in taking possession and living in the land God promised. They must not add or take away any of the Lord's words. The law of God is authoritative, infallible, and true. God's love prompts careful attention to His law. His people are watchful over what their actions convey to the world because they are ambassadors for God. The Israelites will be a discerning and wise nation as they live in a way that honors their Savior. The Israelites will also reflect God's love and righteousness to surrounding pagan nations. But Moses knows the people are inclined to forget. They should not only study the law but also study themselves. Moses states, "Only be on your guard and diligently watch yourselves..." (Deuteronomy 4:9). For the rest of their lives, they must examine their hearts to prevent wandering. Living in God's love is not passive; it is an active resistance to the pull of sin.

Moses remembers the golden calf incident and urges the people to worship God alone. Because they have not seen the form of the invisible God, other than the visible manifestations of His presence, the people will be tempted to return to idolatry. Though the glory of God resides among them, the lack of sight presents a challenge.

They will look at each other, the creatures of the water and air, and the celestial objects and be lured to make idols of these images. Forgetting and rejecting the Creator, the people will raise creatures to divine status and worship them as gods. Moses emphasizes that the Lord has provided these objects as evidence of His power and glory. He is the only one worthy of all worship. The Lord is also jealous. Passionate toward His people and wanting to protect them from harm, God will become angry if they fall into idolatry. Moses then changes this "if" statement to "when." After forty years with them in the wilderness, he knows the people are rebellious and weak. They will succumb to their desires and will be driven out of the Promised Land. Because of their failure to worship God, they will fall to enemy nations and be exiles. But, in His compassion and mercy, the Lord will preserve a remnant and restore them. After all, He is faithful to His covenant promises.

Moses tells the people to consider this unique moment in history. There has been no other time before them when God has done such marvelous acts. He asks:

"Has a people heard God's voice speaking from the fire as you have, and lived? Or has a god attempted to go and take a nation as his own out of another nation, by trials, signs, wonders, and war, by a strong hand and an outstretched arm, by great terrors, as the Lord your God did for you in Egypt before your eyes?" (Deuteronomy 4:33-34)

The Israelites' God is great and all-powerful. There is none other like Him. He graciously rescued the Israelites from Pharaoh and served them in the wilderness. The Lord loves His people. Receiving this love, the people should live with thanksgiving that God chose them with whom to make His covenant. If the Israelites respond in obedience, worship, and gratitude, they will live abundantly with the presence of God in Canaan for all of time.

The Israelites' pattern of behavior throughout the wilderness journey will continue despite the Lord's faithfulness. Like the Israelites, we are naturally bound to our sinful nature and repeat our sin struggles. But the reality of sin does not erase the standard and law that God has for His covenant people. The law is like a mirror showing our brokenness and moral inability. Though called to obey His Word, we are unable to do so in our own capacity. But Jesus, who came as the obedient Son, perfectly kept the law on our behalf. His life, death, and resurrection were the ultimate displays of worship to God the Father. In Him, we are clothed with His goodness which erases the debt of sin. In Jesus, we are also transformed to be new creations with desires and the ability to respond appropriately to God's love. Remain steadfast in obedience, worship, and gratitude, as God gives you the grace to do so.

IN JESUS, WE ARE CLOTHED WITH HIS GOODNESS WHICH ERASES THE DEBT OF SIN.

In what ways could you guard and watch yourself to prevent wandering from God?

_____
_____
_____
_____
_____
_____
_____
_____

How does this passage make you aware of the need to respond in obedience, worship, and gratitude to God's love?

_____
_____
_____
_____
_____
_____
_____

Write out a prayer of thanksgiving for the saving work of Jesus

_____
_____
_____
_____
_____
_____
_____
_____

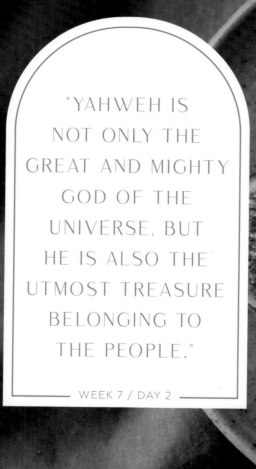

"YAHWEH IS
NOT ONLY THE
GREAT AND MIGHTY
GOD OF THE
UNIVERSE, BUT
HE IS ALSO THE
UTMOST TREASURE
BELONGING TO
THE PEOPLE."

WEEK 7 / DAY 2

Repeating the Shema

Moses teaches the Ten Commandments to the Israelites again. Deuteronomy is a Greek word that means "second law." This book contains a repetition of the commands given at Mount Sinai. Therefore, scholars argue that Moses is leading the people through a covenant renewal ceremony that precedes and marks the beginning of new life in the Promised Land. As seen in yesterday's passage, the Israelites must respond to the love of God by obeying these commands and worshiping the true God alone. Moses expounds on these commands and reveals that the heart motive for such adherence to God's word is love. Their love for the Lord should be the basis for fulfilling the covenant obligations. The Israelites cannot truly thrive in the abundant life that awaits them in Canaan if they do not love the God who first loved them. In this way, keeping the law will not be oppressive or burdensome. Rather, obeying God will pour out of a heart that cherishes and honors the Savior.

Moses's command to love is called the *Shema*. Moses says, "Listen, Israel: The Lord our God, the Lord is one. Love the Lord your God with all your heart, with all your soul, and with all your strength" (Deuteronomy 6:4-5). First, Moses emphasizes the personal relationship between the Israelites and Yahweh. Yahweh is not only the great and mighty God of the universe, but He is also the utmost treasure belonging to the people. The Lord alone must hold this place in their hearts. Affections cannot be divided among other gods, for He is the one true God. Moses calls them to display this love with their entire selves. The heart, which signifies the mind, will, and desires, would overflow with zeal and passion for the Lord. The soul, which points to their principles and beliefs, would have a worldview defined by God's standards. Finally, strength refers to their steadfastness which would give them resolve to be committed to the Lord. Moses urges the people to say, repeat, and write these words wherever they go, so they will be reminded daily. Moses gives the people practical steps to put their love into action. Moses knows the people are difficult, but constant reminders may soften and motivate them to live as covenant people.

Moses's speech anticipates the Promised Land which already contains cities, houses, cisterns, gardens, and vineyards. He emphasizes that people do not have to labor to build anything. The Promised Land is truly a gift. The saving grace of God has freed them from the hands of evil and preserved them through the trial of the wilderness. Now, His grace is bringing them into the richness and fullness of life. In these satisfying times, Moses points out that the Israelites will need to strive to love God even more. The people may grow comfortable, forget, and act in ways that are unloving to God. While beautiful, Canaan is only a picture of the eternal paradise God will establish for His people through His Messiah, the Anointed One who will conquer sin completely (Genesis 3:15). The people are still rebellious, so their possession of Canaan is not secure. Inhabiting Canaan will show where their true treasure lies. Do they value the presence of lush groves more than the presence of God? They must always revere God and seek His righteousness while awaiting the truly righteous Savior and King who will satisfy the law on their behalf and secure them in God's rest forever.

In addition to Canaan, the law is a sign of God's love as well. Moses tells the community they must teach the younger generation "the meaning of the decrees, statutes, and ordinances" that God has commanded (Deuteronomy 6:20). The law is a sign of the Lord's salvation and covenant relationship. In teaching the Shema to their children, the Israelites are to recount the story of Egypt and all the wondrous miracles of God. Remembering through instruction will inspire a love for Him and a love for His law. The people will see God's standard as an extension of His grace as it was established for their peace and prosperity in the land (Deuteronomy 6:24).

In today's passage, we see that God's covenant people are marked by love. The Israelites received God's love through their exodus from Egypt and were called to love Him in return by keeping His law. As believers, we have received the love of God through the salvation of Jesus Christ. This restoring love makes us new and generates belief in our hearts. This sacrificial love accomplishes the law for us and takes the punishment of our sin. This transforming love molds us into the image of our true lover, Jesus. Knowing His love, we are inspired and equipped to love God in the way the Shema invites us to do so. Like the Israelites repeating the Shema, we should continually preach the gospel to ourselves. Read and speak Scripture aloud daily to remind yourself of the great work Jesus accomplished and the call to love God with your whole self.

LIKE THE ISRAELITES REPEATING THE SHEMA, WE SHOULD CONTINUALLY PREACH THE GOSPEL TO OURSELVES.

Identify and write out three imperatives, or command statements, that stick out to you in this passage.

_____

_____

_____

_____

_____

Read John 5:41-44 and 1 John 5:3-5. What is the relationship between receiving the love of God and believing in the saving work of Jesus? Where do faith and love intersect and produce more of each other?

_____

_____

_____

_____

_____

_____

_____

Say and repeat Deuteronomy 6:4-5. Write out a prayer asking for help in loving the Lord with your heart, soul, and strength.

_____

_____

_____

_____

_____

_____

_____

"LEAN ON
JESUS IN TRYING
CIRCUMSTANCES;
HE WILL LEAD
YOU TO THE RICH
LOVE OF GOD."

WEEK 7 / DAY 3

Enduring the Test

The Israelites have reached the end of their test in the wilderness. Because of their sin and grumbling, the people wandered for much longer than what was needed to reach the Promised Land. But, Moses reveals that the Lord has used this time to develop the Israelites. During the forty-year journey, they have witnessed God's faithfulness over and over again. They learned humility and dependence on God. Humility is trust in God's guidance, wisdom, and authority. A humble person recognizes that he or she does not have the moral ability, strength, or understanding to accomplish good for his or her own life. Humility is also submission and service to another, whereas pride is an inflated view of self, denial of weakness, and a sole focus on one's needs. Humans were created to depend on God and submit to His lordship. Moses claims that the Israelites were tested to see what was in their hearts. God knows all and sees into the heart of man. He already knew the Israelites were going to assert pride and not trust in Him. But in His grace and mercy, God wanted His people to know the depths of their sinfulness so that they would look to Him for restoration.

Moses says to the Israelites that the hunger, thirst, scorpions, and snakes all had a purpose and made them lean on God for provision and protection. The Israelites begin to look back at the tough circumstances they faced. They remember the water He brought forth from the rock. They recall the manna the Lord sent from heaven to fill them. Moses claims God brought them to the end of themselves to show them "man does not live on bread alone but on every word that comes from the mouth of God" (Deuteronomy 8:3). The Lord Himself was their sustenance. He kept them from injury and kept their clothes intact. Moses then refers to this test as discipline. Like how a father disciplines his son, the basis for God's discipline is love. God wants His people to be who they were created to be. He wants them to thrive and prosper in union with Him. In parental discipline, the objective is also instruction and reconciliation. Through the wilderness test, the people received lessons on the Lord's character and redemptive plan. After this teaching, the Israelites were brought back into God's embrace with Moses's intercession covering their sin. Because God has their good in mind, Moses follows again with a command to keep God's word. The Israelites can exercise humility and trust in God by obeying His law. In the end, the covenant blessings will follow. The Israelites may be tempted to be prideful and say, "My power and my own ability have gained this wealth for me" (Deuteronomy 8:17). But Moses emphasizes that God is the source and giver of the blessings. The Lord shows His faithfulness to His covenant promises when He blesses the humble.

In Deuteronomy 9, the next part of Moses's speech readies the people to enter the land. Moses stands over the small nation and declares they are about to face a strong and giant people. The Anakim are infamous warriors that no one can defeat. But, the Lord will go before the Israelites and drive the Canaanites out, enacting His righteous judgment on the pagan people. This battle will point forward to the Messiah who will lead God's army in battle against spiritual evil and conquer the serpent. The Israelites should be courageous and excited. God is revealing His redemptive plan through them. Confirming His promise to Abraham, God is establishing a people as His own and reclaiming His kingdom. Despite their sin, God is pre-serving them to bring forth the Promised One who will make the proud humble in Him and, by His righteousness, secure them in the covenant blessings forever.

Though Moses called the people to love and obey, the Israelites continued to fail the test as they did in the wilderness. Moses and subsequent leaders of Israel proved not to be the humble servants of God. But by His faithfulness, God sent His Son, Jesus, who left His divine throne and took on meekness. He was the true, humble servant who exercised complete trust and faith in the Father by obeying His will. Jesus passed the test with excellence, completing the redemptive mission and fulfilling the covenant. Through His life, death, and resurrection, the God of the universe served us, sinners. Jesus bore our guilt and restored us to wholeness in Him. He forgives us of our pride and, by His Spirit, cultivates humility in us. You do not have to travel your journey on your own terms, following the deceitful path of your heart. Lean on Jesus in trying circumstances; He will lead you to the rich love of God.

HE FORGIVES US OF OUR PRIDE AND, BY HIS SPIRIT, CULTIVATES HUMILITY IN US.

What life experiences have tested you?

_____
_____
_____
_____
_____
_____
_____

How did this testing shape your relationship with God?

_____
_____
_____
_____
_____
_____
_____
_____

Identify areas where you have been prideful, and pray for God to reveal
His glory in your weakness.

_____
_____
_____
_____
_____
_____
_____

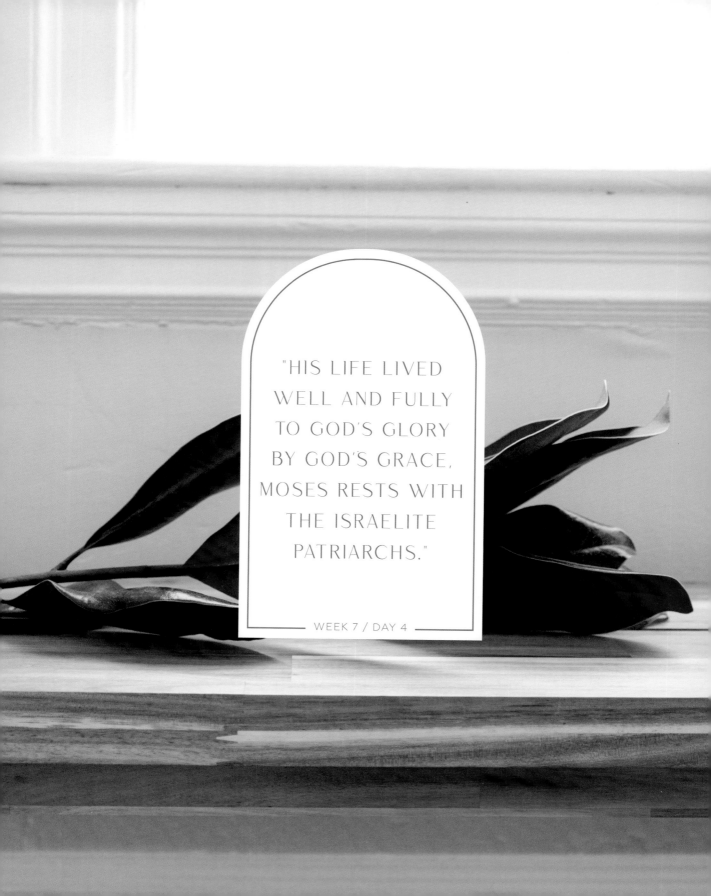

"HIS LIFE LIVED
WELL AND FULLY
TO GOD'S GLORY
BY GOD'S GRACE,
MOSES RESTS WITH
THE ISRAELITE
PATRIARCHS."

WEEK 7 / DAY 4

Resting with Longing

Moses concludes his speech to the Israelites. Now, at 120 years old, Moses is a man of wisdom. Such wisdom is rooted in his life's journey with the Lord. Moses survived genocide as a baby, lived as a prince in Pharaoh's court, was a guilty criminal, worked as a shepherd, witnessed the wondrous miracles of God, led the Israelites through the wilderness, and was the mediator between God and His people. Through it all, God shows him favor. When Moses tells the people to "be strong and courageous" (Deuteronomy 31:6), he speaks from experience. He understands the Lord will not abandon His people. But Moses will not accompany them. He will not cross the Jordan River into Canaan. Because of his unbelief shown at the rock in Numbers 20, Moses is joining the generation of people who will die in the wilderness (Numbers 14:29).

As the Lord commanded, Moses calls Joshua, his assistant, and appoints him to take his leadership position. Joshua's subordinate role has prepared him for this opportunity, though surely he must be hesitant. Before the Israelites, Moses repeats the statement, "be strong and courageous" to Joshua. It seems that Moses is making a visible approval of Joshua's authority so that the whole community knows to submit. Then the Lord tells Moses and Joshua to present themselves at the entrance of the tabernacle. The entrance of the tabernacle is significant as this location indicates the presence of God. The Lord appears in a pillar of cloud and tells Joshua, "I will be with you" (Deuteronomy 31:23). Joshua not only has a divine appointment but also the assurance of the Lord's presence. Through his role as the next chosen leader, Joshua will, like Moses, be blessed by God's nearness. The Lord will enable him to bring the people into the Promised Land and to further God's plan of redemption. Like Moses, Joshua will also point to the coming Savior who will redeem God's people from the bondage of sin, protect them from spiritual evil, make them whole, and live forever with them in His kingdom.

After giving the written law to the elders and the priests, Moses tells them to read these words aloud to the community every seven years. Everyone will hear, learn, and know to obey God's words. This public reading of Scripture will be the customary rhythm for worship as they display God's righteousness in Canaan. But in front of the tabernacle, the Lord confirms Moses's prediction about the people. God reveals that the Israelites will not keep the law and will fall into idolatry again. Then, in the hands of gods who mean them harm and will not protect them, the Israelites will be like prey to enemy nations (Deuteronomy 31:17). God tells Moses to write a song that testifies of the Lord's goodness and the people's sinfulness. The singing will cause the Israelites to remember God's covenant promises. At the end of the song, there is a hope that God will rescue His people from evil and purify them from sin (Deuteronomy 32:43).

The Lord calls Moses to ascend Mount Pisgah. Moses climbs the mountain, reminiscent of when he first met God in the burning bush on Mount Horeb and when he received the Ten Commandments on Mount Sinai. Moses is at the conclusion of his story, and here is where He will rest. Moses gazes over the Promised Land as he is given an opportunity to marvel at the beauty of the landscape and sea. The Lord has graciously allowed him to see Canaan, though he will not enter. In a way, Moses still experiences the gift of the covenant before it is tainted by the Israelites' sin. His life lived well and fully to God's glory by God's grace, Moses rests with the Israelite patriarchs. The Lord personally buries Moses, showing an intimate moment between God and His servant.

Moses was an exemplary leader, but his mediation and faithfulness to God's word only took him and the Israelites so far. The juxtaposition of failure and success and excitement and peace on Mount Pisgah surely leaves Moses longing. Moses died with expectancy and faith in the coming Savior who would restore all things and purify God's people. All of Moses's life points to Him. As Moses took his final breaths, he looked to Jesus, the perfect Son of God sent from heaven who is the true Mediator. This forward hope, not the entrance into Canaan, gave Moses true rest. King Jesus is the Messiah promised in Genesis 3:15 who through His life, death, and resurrection broke the chains of slavery to sin and defeated Satan's rule. Through His obedience, Jesus accomplished the covenant obligations and earned for believers the eternal reward of rest in God's presence. Jesus is the fulfillment of the Promised Land. He atoned for our sin and kept the law of God which we were unable to do so that in Him, we would see the beauty of God and live righteously. Like Moses, we can navigate our life resting in Jesus's salvation while awaiting His second coming when God's promised kingdom will be established on earth.

AS MOSES TOOK HIS FINAL BREATHS, HE LOOKED TO JESUS, THE PERFECT SON OF GOD SENT FROM HEAVEN WHO IS THE TRUE MEDIATOR.

What does Deuteronomy 31:16-21 reveal about God's character?

_____

_____

_____

_____

_____

_____

_____

_____

In what areas of your life do you need to be strong and courageous? Why can you be confident in Jesus?

_____

_____

_____

_____

_____

_____

_____

Summarize how Jesus is the true and better Moses.

_____

_____

_____

_____

_____

_____

_____

_____

"THROUGH OUR FAITH IN HIM, JESUS CARRIED US IN HIS OBEDIENCE."

WEEK 7 / DAY 5

Overcoming the Temptation

In Matthew 4, Jesus's temptation in the wilderness mirrors the Israelites' test during their wilderness journey. Jesus spends forty days and nights there. This time is symbolic of the forty years Israel spent wandering. However, there are also differences. Committing idolatry, the Israelites acted on their sinful nature and failed to worship God. Striking the rock twice, Moses himself lacked trust in the Lord under the stressful circumstances. But, without sin, Jesus faces the serpent and surpasses his temptation. In this way, Jesus proves He is the perfect Son of Man who rightly worships and trusts the Lord.

The Spirit of God moves Jesus into the wilderness where Satan awaits Him. Satan hides in the shadows, watching Jesus as the forty days and nights pass. Jesus does not eat during this time. The physical signs of hunger overtake His body. He likely becomes dizzy and lightheaded, His muscles are tired and shaky. It is probable that His stomach is tied in knots and aches with severe pain while pressure pounds His head. When Satan sees that Jesus is in such a weak condition, he pounces to attack. Satan approaches Jesus with the same tactic he used in the garden of Eden. He tries to sow doubt in Jesus's mind. Satan puts Jesus's identity as the Son of God into question. The tempter attempts to provoke Jesus to assert His power to alleviate His hunger. Jesus is in a worse physical condition than the Israelites were, but instead of grumbling, He responds with God's Word. Jesus quotes Moses from Deuteronomy 8:3. He says, "It is written: Man must not live on bread alone but on every word that comes from the mouth of God" (Matthew 4:4). Jesus will not turn stones into bread for Himself, but He will trust in God for sustenance and provision. Satan then takes Jesus to the top of the temple in Jerusalem and tries to get Him to jump. Quoting Psalm 91:11-12, Satan misuses God's Word to test God's protection. Jesus responds with Deuteronomy 6:16: "Do not test the Lord your God" (Matthew 4:7). Jesus remains humble and does not presume upon the Father. Then the tempter takes Jesus to a high mountain and shows Him a vision of all the kingdoms. Satan tries to appeal to common human desires for possession. Satan claims that all the kingdoms will belong to Jesus if Jesus will bow down and worship him. Jesus's final response is a passionate rejection of idolatry. Jesus rebukes Satan and recites Deuteronomy 6:13: "Go away, Satan! For it is written: Worship the Lord your God, and serve only him" (Matthew 4:10). Jesus accomplishes what Adam and Eve, Moses, and the Israelites could not do. He overcomes Satan and sends him away. Jesus passes through the wilderness, temple, and mountain testing, worshiping God and revealing He is the Promised One.

Through our faith in Him, Jesus carried us in His obedience. As the true Mediator, Jesus represented believers as He overcame Satan's temptation so that in Him, we, sinners, would be seen as God's righteous worshipers. Jesus explains this integral dependence on Him in John 15:1-17. Using garden imagery, Jesus claims He is the vine, and we are branches. A vine and its branches are structurally linked. Though they are different parts, the vine and branches are essentially one living organism. The vine primarily possesses nutrients overflowing into the branches. The branches are dependent on the vine for nutrients and growth. A branch produces fruit because of its organic connection to the vine. A branch cannot produce fruit if it is on its own. Like a branch to a vine, we are connected to our Savior, Jesus, through faith in Him. We are dependent on Him for life in God's presence. We must abide in Him for our sins to be forgiven and to be restored from Satan's harm. By God's grace through faith, Moses and the Israelites who looked forward to the coming Savior were covered in Jesus's obedience. Though failing in the wilderness, they passed the test because of the saving work of Jesus. Despite our sin and falling to Satan's scheme, the tempter does not have ultimate victory over us. The true Mediator has endured suffering in the wilderness and took our punishment on the cross so that we could be free from guilt. United to Him, we produce the fruit of Jesus's righteousness. As a result, we love God and one another. As we saw in the Deuteronomy passages this week, there is a call for God's people to love. But, on our own, we are not able to love God and others. Apart from the vine, we are not able to exercise our love in obedience. But, if we remain in the sacrificial love of Jesus, we can produce the type of love that seeks to resist evil, serve the weak, heal the wounded, and redeem the oppressed.

LIKE A BRANCH TO A VINE, WE ARE CONNECTED TO OUR SAVIOR, JESUS, THROUGH FAITH IN HIM. WE ARE DEPENDENT ON HIM FOR LIFE IN GOD'S PRESENCE.

How does God use Satan's ploy for His redemptive purposes?

_____

_____

_____

_____

_____

_____

_____

_____

_____

Read 1 Timothy 2:5, Hebrews 4:15, and Hebrews 2:17. What insight do these verses bring to Jesus's temptation story?

_____

_____

_____

_____

_____

_____

_____

_____

What can you do to abide in the love of God?

_____

_____

_____

_____

_____

_____

_____

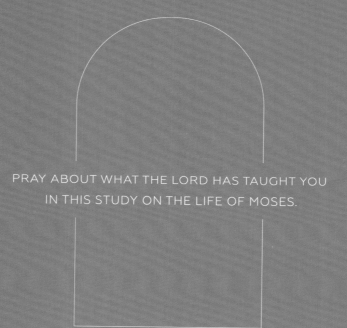

PRAY ABOUT WHAT THE LORD HAS TAUGHT YOU
IN THIS STUDY ON THE LIFE OF MOSES.

LORD, YOU HAVE BEEN OUR REFUGE IN EVERY GENERATION. BEFORE THE MOUNTAINS WERE BORN, BEFORE YOU GAVE BIRTH TO THE EARTH AND THE WORLD, FROM ETERNITY TO ETERNITY, YOU ARE GOD.

Psalm 90:1-2
a psalm by Moses

Week 07 Reflection

Summarize the main points from this week's Scripture readings.

_____
_____
_____
_____
_____
_____
_____
_____
_____
_____
_____
_____

What did you observe from this week's passages about God and His character?

_____
_____
_____
_____
_____
_____
_____
_____
_____
_____
_____
_____

What do this week's passages reveal about the condition of mankind and yourself?

_____
_____
_____
_____
_____
_____

How do these passages point to the gospel?

_____

_____

_____

_____

_____

How should you respond to these Scriptures? What specific action steps can you take this week to apply them in your life?

Write a prayer in response to your study of God's Word. Adore God for who He is, confess sins that He revealed in your own life, ask Him to empower you to walk in obedience, and pray for anyone who comes to mind as you study.

What is the Gospel?

THANK YOU FOR READING AND ENJOYING THIS STUDY WITH US! WE ARE ABUNDANTLY GRATEFUL FOR THE WORD OF GOD, THE INSTRUCTION WE GLEAN FROM IT, AND THE EVER-GROWING UNDERSTANDING ABOUT GOD'S CHARACTER FROM IT. WE ARE ALSO THANKFUL THAT SCRIPTURE CONTINUALLY POINTS TO ONE THING IN INNUMERABLE WAYS: THE GOSPEL.

We remember our brokenness when we read about the fall of Adam and Eve in the garden of Eden (Genesis 3), when sin entered into a perfect world and maimed it. We remember the necessity that something innocent must die to pay for our sin when we read about the atoning sacrifices in the Old Testament. We read that we have all sinned and fallen short of the glory of God (Romans 3:23) and that the penalty for our brokenness, the wages of our sin, is death (Romans 6:23). We all are in need of grace and mercy, but most importantly, we all need a Savior.

We consider the goodness of God when we realize that He did not plan to leave us in this dire state. We see His promise to buy us back from the clutches of sin and death in Genesis 3:15. And we see that promise accomplished with Jesus Christ on the cross. Jesus Christ knew no sin yet became sin so that we might become righteous through His sacrifice (2 Corinthians 5:21). Jesus was tempted in every way that we are and lived sinlessly. He was reviled yet still yielded Himself for our sake, that we may have life abundant in Him. Jesus lived the perfect life that we could not live and died the death that we deserved.

The gospel is profound yet simple. There are many mysteries in it that we can never exhaust this side of heaven, but there is still overwhelming weight to its implications in this life. The gospel is the telling of our sinfulness and God's goodness, and this gracious gift compels a response. We are saved by grace through faith, which means that we rest with faith in the grace that Jesus Christ displayed on the cross (Ephesians 2:8-9). We cannot save ourselves from our brokenness or do any amount of good works to merit God's favor, but we can have faith that what Jesus accomplished in His death, burial, and resurrection was more than enough for our salvation and our eternal delight. When we accept God, we are commanded to die to our self and our sinful desires and live a life worthy of the calling we have received (Ephesians 4:1). The gospel compels us to be sanctified, and in so doing, we are conformed to the likeness of Christ Himself. This is hope. This is redemption. This is the gospel.

SCRIPTURE TO REFERENCE:

GENESIS 3:15   *I will put hostility between you and the woman, and between your offspring and her offspring. He will strike your head, and you will strike his heel.*

ROMANS 3:23   *For all have sinned and fall short of the glory of God.*

ROMANS 6:23   *For the wages of sin is death, but the gift of God is eternal life in Christ Jesus our Lord.*

2 CORINTHIANS 5:21   *He made the one who did not know sin to be sin for us, so that in him we might become the righteousness of God.*

EPHESIANS 2:8-9   *For you are saved by grace through faith, and this is not from yourselves; it is God's gift — not from works, so that no one can boast.*

EPHESIANS 4:1   *Therefore I, the prisoner in the Lord, urge you to walk worthy of the calling you have received,*

"

Jesus is the fulfillment of the
Promised Land. He atoned for our
sin and kept the law of God which
we were unable to do so that in
Him, we would see the beauty of
God and live righteously.

"

Thank you for studying
God's Word with us!

CONNECT WITH US
@thedailygraceco
@kristinschmucker

CONTACT US
info@thedailygraceco.com

SHARE
#thedailygraceco
#lampandlight

VISIT US ONLINE
thedailygraceco.com

MORE DAILY GRACE
The Daily Grace App
Daily Grace Podcast